JO WHEATLEY
HOME BAKING

Jo Wheatley
Home Baking

CONSTABLE

For my nan, where it all began

Constable & Robinson Ltd
55–56 Russell Square
London WC1B 4HP
www.constablerobinson.com

First published in Great Britain in 2013 by Constable,
an imprint of Constable & Robinson Ltd.
This printed paper cased edition published in 2014 by Constable.

Text copyright © Jo Wheatley, 2013
Photographs © Martin Poole, 2013

The moral right of the author has been asserted.

A CIP catalogue record for this book
is available from the British Library.

ISBN 978-1-47210-935-4 (hardback)
ISBN 978-1-47211-716-8 (PPC)

Design & art direction: Smith & Gilmour
Food stylists: Annie Rigg & Kim Morphew
Prop stylist: Lydia Brun

Printed and bound in Italy

INTRODUCTION

For me baking is about memories: old ones, new ones and ones yet to be made. I love how the smell of fresh bread baking can give you that cosy feeling and for me, there's nothing more welcoming than entering the house of someone who's baking. I made biscuits the other day and it took me straight back to when I'd bake chocolate chip and peanut butter cookies almost daily for the boys and their friends.

Baking creates traditions, too. Whether it's a Christmas cake recipe from an old cookery book that you have tailored into something unique for your family – I'm not a huge lover of currants so I add dried apricots and cranberries to mine – or a birthday cake that you made for a special someone. Or even a simple shortbread that you can make with your eyes closed.

I have thought hard about what I'd like to include in this my second baking book, and have listened to what you've asked for on my Facebook and Twitter pages, too. As in *A Passion for Baking*, I've tried to keep most of the recipes to one page, using everyday ingredients, and included lots of pictures. I know myself I find nothing more off-putting than huge amounts of text, lots of fancy, hard-to-source ingredients and, worst of all, no picture of the finished bake.

I have really enjoyed developing the recipes for this book. I have so many foil-wrapped parcels in my freezer that it looks like Metal Mickey's wardrobe (now I'm showing my age!). But it's definitely better than wasting all that food, so we are now well stocked for the rest of the year!

When I started writing *Home Baking*, I wanted to add a chapter on easy supper dishes that could be mainly baked in one pan. I wanted the recipes to involve as little fuss as possible and hardly any washing up! This is my sort of cooking – big flavours with minimum effort. The recipes in the Supper Bakes chapter work really well for mid-week family teas but are equally great for an informal supper party. Just let the oven do the work while you entertain your guests.

As you can tell, I love food. I spend most of my time talking about it, thinking about it and making it. I even have the body to prove it. What's that saying? 'Never trust a skinny cook.' Well, I think that is my mantra.

And I love what writing about it has given me. Developing new recipes and sharing them with you has increased my passion for baking more than I thought was possible. It's like a light switch has been flicked on for my tastebuds and I've found excitement in every new flavour and bake, adding twists to old favourites and finding new ones.

For those who know me, you'll be aware that to my deep disappointment I left school without very good grades. So, to be writing my second book gives me such a feeling of pride and self worth. It's something I'd have never dreamed I would accomplish. It does just prove, though, that you never know what's around the corner, and the only opportunities to be sad about are the ones you don't take.

I hope that you will all love *Home Baking* as much as I do.

Jo x

Chapter
one

BISCUITS,
BARS AND
COOKIES

*Crisp buttery biscuits, chewy giant cookies, sticky bars
of delight. These are all recipes of things I've tried along
the way, decided I needed to make my own and now want
to share with you. Time to pop the kettle on and join me
for one or two of these irresistible treats.*

CHILLI CHOCOLATE COOKIES

These were a happy accident – crisp on the outside, chewy in the middle and then with a surprising tickle from the chilli.

**40g good-quality dark
  chocolate, chopped**
½ tsp chilli flakes
50g caster sugar
100g plain flour
½ tsp bicarbonate of soda
70g unsalted butter, softened
50g brown sugar
2 tbsp golden syrup

Decoration
30g white chocolate, chopped

**You will also need 3 large
baking trays lined with
baking parchment and
a microwaveable plastic
sandwich bag**

TOP TIP
If you don't have a pestle and
mortar, you can still crush the
chilli and sugar together in
a mug or small bowl using
the end of a rolling pin.

Melt the dark chocolate either in a heatproof bowl over a pan of barely simmering water or in the microwave on a low setting in 20-second bursts. Set to one side and leave to cool slightly.

Grind the chilli flakes and a pinch of the caster sugar together with a pestle and mortar until you have a fine powder.

Put all of the remaining ingredients in the bowl of a food processor and blend until combined. Add the melted chocolate and chilli sugar and pulse until the mixture comes together.

Roll into 12–15 small balls and flatten slightly on to the three baking trays – 4 or 5 on each tray as they will spread.

Freeze or chill for half an hour until firm while you preheat the oven to 170°C/325°C/Gas Mark 3.

Bake on the middle shelf of the oven for 15–18 minutes. Leave to cool on the tray for 5 minutes before carefully transferring to a wire rack to cool completely.

To decorate, melt the white chocolate in the sandwich bag in the microwave on a low setting in 10-second bursts. Snip the end off the bag and drizzle the white chocolate over the cooled biscuits.

OAT, PECAN AND RAISIN COOKIES

A great thing to pop into lunchboxes. Providing a slow release of energy,
these cookies are also perfect for that mid-morning snack.

170g unsalted butter, softened
320g soft light brown sugar
1 large egg, beaten
4 tbsp sunflower oil
250g plain flour
½ tsp bicarbonate of soda
½ tsp ground cinnamon
150g rolled oats
150g raisins
150g pecans, roughly chopped

You will also need 2–3
baking sheets lined with
baking parchment

Preheat the oven to 180°C/350°F/Gas Mark 4.

In the bowl of a free-standing mixer, cream together the butter and sugar until pale and light. If you don't have a free-standing mixer you can use an electric hand-held mixer. Add the egg and oil and mix again. Sift the flour, bicarbonate of soda and cinnamon into the bowl, add the oats, raisins and chopped pecans and mix again until smooth and thoroughly combined.

Using your hands, roll the cookie dough into walnut-sized balls and place on the prepared baking sheets. Allow plenty of space between each cookie as they will spread during baking. Slightly flatten them with the palm of your hand and bake on the middle shelf of the preheated oven for about 20 minutes until pale golden and firm.

Remove from baking sheets and cool on wire racks.

MY TAKE ON MARYLANDS

Hazelnuts remind me of being a child at Christmas – the satisfaction you got when a whole hazelnut stayed intact! The good thing about having to crack the shells yourself was that you'd only ever eat a few after an eternity of cracking. The recipe for the Maryland cookies that you can buy in the shops is a closely-guarded secret, so my take on them is a deliciously chocolatey and nutty shortbread, perfect for dunking in a mug of tea.

**50g good-quality dark
    chocolate, roughly chopped**
**50g hazelnuts, plus 25 extra,
    to decorate**
100g unsalted butter, softened
70g caster sugar
**150g plain flour, plus extra
    for dusting**

**You will also need 2 large
baking trays lined with
baking parchment**

Melted chocolate
For an extra embellishment you
could always drizzle over a little
melted milk chocolate. Try my
melt-in-a-bag trick from page 249.

Blitz the dark chocolate and 50g hazelnuts together in a food processor until the size of breadcrumbs. Remove and set to one side.

Cream together the butter and sugar in the food processor until pale, light and fluffy. Add the chocolate, hazelnuts and flour and pulse until the mixture comes together to form a ball.

Lightly dust the work surface with flour and roll out the dough into a 2.5cm diameter log, wrap in clingfilm and chill for 30 minutes then cut into 2.5cm discs. Arrange the biscuits on the baking trays, leaving a 3cm gap between each.

Press a hazelnut firmly into each disc so they are well embedded, and place the trays in the fridge to chill while you preheat the oven to 170ºC/325ºF/Gas Mark 3.

Bake the chilled biscuits on the middle shelf of the preheated oven for 12–15 minutes. Keep an eye on the biscuits for the last few minutes to make sure they don't burn. Leave on the tray to cool for 5 minutes before transferring the cookies to a wire rack until cold.

ANZAC COOKIES

A few months ago I went to a really lovely restaurant in Battersea.
It was facing the river and they had an amazing table of baked goodies
and my favourite Illy coffee. I hadn't ever tried these biscuits before,
but they were really good and so here's my version.

80g plain flour
100g rolled oats
60g desiccated coconut
80g unsalted butter
2 tbsp golden syrup
60g caster sugar
½ tsp bicarbonate of soda
1 tsp hot water

You will also need 2
baking trays lined with
baking parchment

Preheat the oven to 170°C/325°F/Gas Mark 3.

In a large bowl, mix together the flour, oats and coconut.

Tip the butter, golden syrup and sugar into a medium-sized saucepan and, stirring constantly, melt over a low heat. Add the dry ingredients.

Mix together the bicarbonate of soda and hot water, and add to the mixture. Stir everything together until combined, then shape into walnut-sized balls.

Pat each ball down slightly on to the lined baking trays, leaving a 5cm gap between each. Bake on the middle shelf of the preheated oven for 10 minutes until slightly spread and golden.

Leave to cool on the tray for 5 minutes before transferring the cookies to a wire rack to cool completely.

HONEYCOMB BARS

Everyone who knows me will testify that I have a massive coffee addiction. I'm often to be found with a large two-handled coffee cup containing a skinny cappuccino. Anyway, I recently popped into Costa and they were selling these squares. I liked them so much I decided to try and make my own version.

100g unsalted butter, melted
25g soft brown sugar
3 tbsp cocoa powder
4 tbsp golden syrup
400g milk chocolate
200g digestive biscuits
8 Crunchie bars

You will also need a 30 x 23cm baking tin with a depth of about 4cm, lightly greased and lined with baking paper

TOP TIP
To make the bars easier to cut, keep a mug of boiling water nearby when slicing the squares, to warm the knife.

Put the melted butter, sugar, cocoa powder and golden syrup into a large bowl and mix together with a wooden spoon until well combined.

Break the chocolate into pieces and melt in a heatproof bowl over barely simmering water.

Place the digestive biscuits and Crunchie bars in a sandwich bag and roughly crush with a rolling pin until you have bite-sized shards in a variety of different shapes. Add to the bowl and mix together to combine.

Spoon into the lined tin, press down firmly into all the corners and top with the melted chocolate.

Chill for half an hour or until nearly set, then slice into bars with a hot knife. Return to the fridge to firm completely.

PARMESAN, CHILLI AND ROSEMARY BISCUITS

I love the saltiness of the Parmesan and the pungent woodiness that comes from the rosemary in these savoury biscuits. They're perfect to serve on a platter with cheese and grapes.

100g unsalted butter, softened
100g Parmesan, finely grated
1 large egg
150g plain flour
25g polenta/fine cornmeal
pinch of dried rosemary
pinch of dried chilli flakes

You will also need a large baking tray lined with baking parchment

TOP TIP
If you want you could freeze the unbaked biscuits in bags in the freezer for up to 3 months.

Put the butter and grated Parmesan in the bowl of a food processor and blitz to combine. Add the egg and pulse until combined.

Add the plain flour, polenta, rosemary and chilli and pulse in the machine until just combined. Turn out on to a lightly floured work surface and bring together into a sausage shape, 3cm in diameter. Cover and chill for 30 minutes. Slice into 1cm thick rounds and place on the prepared baking sheet.

Chill the biscuits for at least half an hour while you preheat the oven to 170°C/325°F/Gas Mark 3.

Bake the biscuits on the middle shelf of the preheated oven for 15–18 minutes. Transfer to a wire rack to cool.

SPICED ORANGE AND CRANBERRY BISCUITS

Orange and cranberry remind me of holidaying in the Med. As I'm not a big drinker, this 'mocktail' was about as exotic as it got, but ever since then I've loved these two flavours mixed together.

100g unsalted butter, softened
70g caster sugar
finely grated zest of 1 orange
150g plain flour
1 heaped tsp mixed spice
50g dried cranberries

You will also need a baking tray lined with baking parchment and a 6cm round cutter

TOP TIP
I always roll out my biscuits, and often pastry, between two sheets of baking parchment. This means that you don't have to add any extra flour, so the biscuits won't be tough and the work surface will stay clean!

Cream together the butter, sugar and orange zest in the bowl of a food processor until light and fluffy.

Add the flour and spice and pulse until it comes together to form a ball.

Tip the mixture onto a sheet of baking parchment. Place another layer of parchment on top and roll the mixture out to a thickness of 1cm. Cut out into 6cm discs and place on the lined baking tray. Stud with 4-5 cranberries per biscuit.

Chill for 1 hour or until firm. Preheat the oven to 170°C/325°F/Gas Mark 3.

Bake the biscuits on the middle shelf of the preheated oven for 14-18 minutes. Leave to cool on the baking tray for 5 minutes before transferring to a wire rack to cool completely.

OATY FRUIT SQUARES

I love the stickiness of dried fruits, which, when combined with oats and seeds, make really tasty and moist, chewy squares. I used to prepare these in the evening and chill them overnight so they were really firm, and ready for the kids' lunchboxes in the morning.

250g unsalted butter
175g soft light brown sugar
150g golden syrup
350g oats
50g pumpkin seeds
20g sesame seeds
100g dried apricots
100g dried figs
50g dried dates

You will also need a 20cm square baking tin lined with baking parchment

Preheat the oven to 160°C/300°F/Gas Mark 2.

In a large saucepan, melt the butter, sugar and syrup together over a gentle heat. Let the mixture bubble and reduce until thickened and syrupy.

Meanwhile roughly chop the dried apricots, figs and dates and mix to combine.

Combine the oats and seeds in a large bowl. Pour over the syrup and give the mixture a good stir with a wooden spoon. Take half the mixture and press into the lined baking tray.

Spread the chopped and mixed fruit in an even layer over the oat bars and top with the remaining oats and seeds mixture. Press down firmly.

Bake in the preheated oven for 20 minutes or until golden brown and starting to firm at the edges.

Remove from the oven and roughly mark out the squares while still warm. Leave to cool completely in the tin for at least 3-4 hours before serving.

TRIPLE-CHOCOLATE COOKIES

With three boys, you can't imagine the amount of cookies I go through – it always seemed to be our house where hordes of boys congregated. My friends would turn up with a car full of boys and go home alone. I got used to hearing, 'Mum, can so and so stay tonight?' so it pays to have a batch of these on standby for when you have unexpected young guests. The thing with boys, though, is they can never sit quietly when there is mischief to be had.

200g unsalted butter, softened

325g light soft brown sugar

2 large eggs, beaten

1 tsp vanilla extract or vanilla bean paste

400g plain flour

1 tsp baking powder

1 tsp bicarbonate of soda

pinch of sea salt

70g dark chocolate, chopped into small chunks

70g milk chocolate, chopped into small chunks

70g white chocolate, chopped into small chunks

You will also need 2–3 baking sheets lined with baking parchment

Preheat the oven to 170ºC/325ºF/Gas Mark 3.

Cream the butter and sugar together in the bowl of a free-standing mixer until pale, light and fluffy. If you don't have a free-standing mixer you can use an electric hand whisk. Gradually add the beaten eggs, mixing well between each addition. Scrape down the sides of the bowl with a rubber spatula, add the vanilla and mix again.

Sift the flour, baking powder, bicarbonate of soda and salt into the bowl and mix again until thoroughly combined.

Fold the three chocolates into the cookie dough.

Use an ice-cream scoop or large spoon to scoop out the dough in even-sized mounds. Place 3–4 cookies on each baking sheet, allowing plenty of space inbetween as they will spread during cooking.

Bake the cookies in batches on the middle shelf of the preheated oven for about 5 minutes. Remove from the oven and sharply bang the baking tray on the work surface to deflate the cookies and then return to the oven for a further 5–7 minutes until pale golden brown.

Allow the cookies to cool on the baking sheets for 5 minutes before transferring to wire racks until cold.

SHORTBREAD

Shortbread is a favourite of my brother George. This is the simple, classic recipe, but there are so many variations to try, from almond to citrus zest. Have fun with it!

100g plain flour
50g cornflour
100g unsalted butter, softened
50g caster sugar, plus extra
   for sprinkling

You will also need an 18cm loose-bottomed sandwich tin, greased and lined with baking parchment

Preheat the oven to 170°C/325°C/Gas Mark 3.

Tip all the ingredients into the bowl of a food processor and pulse until the mixture comes together to form a soft, clay-like dough. Press firmly into the lined tin in an even layer.

Bake on the middle shelf of the preheated oven for 30–35 minutes until the shortbread is a pale golden colour.

Sprinkle with caster sugar and leave to cool for 10 minutes in the tin. Mark out eight triangle portions, then leave to cool completely before serving.

Bits & Bobs

Flavoured shortbread
See page 248 for some simple ideas to add a touch of flavour.

Chapter
two

BREAD AND SCONES

*For me, breads are a staple, and once you have a good
basic bread dough – warm and silky soft – you will own
it forever. To be able to recreate a fantastic bread time
and time again is a wonderful thing. Two things I would
say: firstly, no two bags of flour are ever the same, so bear
this in mind because small variations can make your
dough behave in very different ways during the kneading
and proving stages. You want a nice soft dough; if it feels
too tight, then it probably is, so add a little more liquid.
Secondly, remember that the time required for proving
may vary depending on factors such as the temperature
of your kitchen and the amount of dough in the bowl.
A recipe can say an hour, but when you touch your dough
it should gently spring back into shape once it's ready,
so trust your own judgement instead of sticking rigidly
to timings. When shaping your bread, make sure you
pull and tuck the dough under so that it forms a taut
ball – this will ensure it rises upwards rather than
outwards. The main thing to remember with scones
is to never overwork them or they will, without
doubt, be tough and rubbery.*

SEEDED WHITE BREAD

This little bread is a fast prover. I use oil and water, and it will lend itself to any seeds, nuts or flour topping. Be adventurous: once you have conquered the basic dough you can adapt with any topping you like. The honey acts as a natural sweetener.

500g strong white bread flour, plus extra for kneading

7g easy-blend/fast-action yeast

50g mixed seeds (try sesame, pumpkin, linseed and sunflower)

8g sea salt

320ml warm water

1 dessertspoon clear, runny honey

You will also need a baking tray and a wooden proving basket, optional

Mix together the flour, yeast, seeds and salt in a free-standing mixer fitted with a dough hook, or in a large bowl with a wooden spoon or spatula, and make a well in the centre.

Mix the water and honey together, add to the dry ingredients and mix on a slow-medium speed to form a rough dough. Continue to knead in the machine for 6 minutes, or by hand for 10 minutes, until the dough is smooth and elastic.

Shape the dough into a ball and place in a large, lightly oiled bowl. Cover with cling film and leave in a warm place to prove for about 1 hour or until doubled in size.

Tip out the dough onto a lightly floured work surface and knead for a further 30 seconds to knock back the dough. Mould it into a round, or any shape you like, cover with oiled cling film and leave to prove for another hour or until the dough has doubled in size and feels springy.

Preheat the oven to 220°C/400°F/Gas Mark 6.

Dust the baking tray and the loaf lightly with flour and bake in the middle of the oven for 25–30 minutes until golden brown and the underside of the loaf sounds hollow when tapped.

Let the loaf cool on the tray for 10 minutes before turning out onto a wire rack. Leave to cool before slicing.

BLUEBERRY BRIOCHE ROLLS

A few years ago, I went to stay with Richard's brother and his wife in France. Every morning my sister-in-law would buy these gorgeous pastries from a local bakery. I always nabbed a billowing soft brioche crowned with sugar nibs. It brightened my morning. The dough for this recipe can be a little wet and so, if you have the option, make it in a free-standing mixer.

500g strong white bread flour,
   plus extra for kneading
7g easy-blend/fast-action yeast
7g sea salt
1 tbsp caster sugar
80ml full-fat milk
120ml water
70g unsalted butter
finely grated zest of 1 orange
3 large eggs
2 large egg yolks
2 (roughly 360g) punnets
   of blueberries
1 egg, beaten with 1 tbsp milk
sugar nibs or crushed sugar
   cubes (see Top Tip below)

You will also need 2–3 baking trays, lined with baking parchment, or 24 individual brioche tins

TOP TIP
Sugar nibs are available from specialist food retailers, online and bigger supermarkets with a decent baking section, but if you can't find sugar nibs, roughly crush sugar cubes using a rolling pin to create the same effect.

Tip the flour, yeast, salt and sugar into the bowl of a free-standing mixer fitted with a dough hook, or a large mixing bowl. Mix together to combine and make a well in the centre.

Heat the milk and water together over a low heat until warm, then stir in the butter and orange zest until melted; slowly add to the dry ingredients. Stir in one egg at a time until all the eggs and yolks have been incorporated.

Knead for 7 minutes in the machine or 12 minutes by hand, cover with oiled cling film and leave to prove in a warm place for 90 minutes or until doubled in size.

Turn out onto a lightly floured work surface and knead for 30 seconds to knock back the dough. Divide into 24 small balls, push 3 or 4 blueberries into the middle of each ball and shape as desired and place on baking trays, or put into individual brioche tins. Allow to prove for a further hour.

Preheat the oven to 190ºC/375ºF/Gas Mark 5.

Brush each roll with the beaten egg and milk and top with the sugar nibs. Bake in the preheated oven for 10–12 minutes until golden.

SPELT BREAD

In the last year, baking bread has truly become my passion. I really enjoy trying out new flavours and techniques and I love the nutty wholesome flavour spelt adds to this bread; just bear in mind that spelt takes a little longer to prove. Sliced finely, this bread is delicious for a smoked salmon sandwich with lemon mayo and rocket.

275g strong white bread flour,
   plus extra for kneading
175g spelt flour
7g easy-blend/fast-action yeast
8g sea salt
100ml full-fat milk
200ml water
1 dessertspoon clear,
   runny honey
25g unsalted butter, melted
1 egg yolk, beaten

You will also need a 900g (2lb)
loaf tin, lightly greased

Tip the dry ingredients into the bowl of a free-standing mixer fitted with a dough hook, or a large mixing bowl, and make a well in the centre.

Heat the milk, water and honey together until lukewarm. Add the melted butter and stir to combine.

Pour into the dry ingredients and combine using the mixer running on a slow to medium speed or with a wooden spoon or spatula until the dough comes together. Continue to knead for 7 minutes using the machine or 10–12 minutes by hand until you have a smooth, elastic dough.

Shape into a ball and place in a large, lightly oiled bowl; cover with oiled cling film and leave in a warm place for 1 ½ - 2 hours or until doubled in size.

Turn out onto a lightly floured work surface and knead for 1 minute to knock back the dough. Mould it into a neat sausage shape and pop into the loaf tin; cover with oiled cling film and leave to prove for 40 minutes to 1 hour until the dough has doubled in size and feels springy.

Preheat the oven to 200ºC/400ºF/Gas Mark 6.

Gently brush the top of the loaf with the beaten egg and bake just below the middle of the oven for 25–30 minutes until golden brown and the underside of the loaf sounds hollow when tapped.

Cool the loaf in the tin for 10 minutes and then turn out onto a wire rack. Leave until cold before slicing.

FOCACCIA

This bread was my biggest joy while filming The Great British Bake Off. *Everyone except myself and Yasmin had these huge hunks of focaccia – ours looked thin and misshapen. To add insult to injury, we had to wait until the next morning to be judged. We went back to the hotel feeling very disheartened, only to find our two were placed first and second. Paul told me mine was one of the best he'd tried in a long time: high praise indeed! This is a really wet dough, so use a free-standing mixer if possible, and add the water slowly.*

300g strong white bread flour,
plus extra for kneading
7g easy-blend/fast-action yeast
10g sea salt
250ml warm water
olive oil, for kneading
fresh rosemary sprigs
4 tbsp rosemary oil or extra
virgin olive oil

You will also need a Swiss
roll sized baking tin, lightly
greased and lined with
baking parchment

Rosemary oil
See page 248 for how to make
your own rosemary-infused oil.

In the bowl of a free-standing mixer, or a large mixing bowl, combine the flour, yeast and 6g of the salt. Slowly add the water, a third at a time. The dough will be very wet, almost the consistency of thick wallpaper paste, so don't be alarmed!

Turn it out onto a well-oiled work surface. Oil your hands and knead the dough for about 5 minutes. If you are using a machine fitted with a dough hook, reduce the time to 3 minutes.

Put the dough back into the cleaned, lightly oiled bowl, cover with cling film and leave to prove for 1 hour until it has doubled in size.

Tip out onto the work surface and knead for 30 seconds to knock back the dough.

Using your hands press the dough into the Swiss roll tin to a thickness of about 1cm. Use your fingers to make small indentations in the dough. Cover with oiled cling film and leave to prove for a further hour.

Preheat the oven to 220°C/425°F/Gas Mark 7.

Bake for 30 minutes in the centre of the oven, then remove and sprinkle over the remaining salt; press in the rosemary sprigs and drizzle with the rosemary oil. Return to the oven for a final 5 minutes.

Cool the bread in the tin for 10 minutes before transferring onto a wire rack.

Bread and scones

GROUND CINNAMON BUNS

Cream cheese frosting, a ground cinnamon-flavoured filling and soft, fluffy melt-in-the-mouth dough… I could honestly get through at least half a tray on my own.

450g strong white bread flour,
    plus extra for kneading
7g easy-blend/fast-action yeast
10g sea salt
125ml full-fat milk
40g unsalted butter
1 tbsp clear, runny honey
175ml tepid water

Filling
100g unsalted butter, melted
100g demerara sugar
3 tsp ground cinnamon

Icing
100g unsalted butter
200g icing sugar
1 tsp ground cinnamon
100g full-fat cream cheese

You will also need a 12-hole muffin tin, lightly buttered

TOP TIP
Make the icing by whisking together the butter, icing sugar and cinnamon until light and fluffy. Add the cream cheese but be careful not to overwhip or the icing will split. Spread the icing over the warm buns using a palette knife.

Tip the flour into the bowl of a free-standing mixer fitted with a dough hook; add the yeast and salt and make a well in the centre. Heat the milk, water and butter in a small saucepan until lukewarm and the butter has melted. Add the honey and pour into the dry ingredients.

Mix together until you have a soft dough. Knead in the mixer for 6 minutes, or by hand for 10 minutes, until the dough is smooth and elastic.

Shape into a ball and put into a large oiled mixing bowl. Cover with cling film and leave in a warm place for 90 minutes or until doubled in size.

Turn out onto a lightly floured work surface and knead for 30 seconds to knock back the dough. Roll into a large, neat 1cm thick rectangle and brush liberally with the melted butter. Mix together the demerera sugar and cinnamon and sprinkle over the dough.

With the long side of the rectangle nearest to you, roll the dough away from you into a tight spiral. Brush the end with a little melted butter to seal. Trim off the ends and slice into 9 equal portions. Pop the buns into the buttered muffin tin, cut-side uppermost, cover loosely with oiled cling film and leave to prove for 40 minutes or until doubled in size.

Preheat the oven to 200°C/400°F/Gas Mark 6.

Bake the buns on the middle shelf of the oven for 20–25 minutes until well risen and golden brown. Cool for 10–15 minutes in the tin and then turn out onto to a wire rack.

CHEESY TEAR AND SHARE

A restaurant we love to go to serves delicious little cheesy rolls to start, with a dish of balsamic vinegar and another of extra virgin olive oil to dip them in. Well, here's my version.

500g strong white bread flour
7g easy-blend/fast-action yeast
8g sea salt
10g caster sugar
10g unsalted butter, softened
handful of picked herbs,
  such as rosemary,
  thyme and oregano
2 garlic cloves
120ml hot water
200ml cold full-fat milk
1 large egg
100g mozzarella, grated
150g Gruyère, grated
1 egg, beaten with 1 tbsp milk

You will also need two baking trays, lightly greased and lined with baking parchment

Tip the flour, yeast, salt and sugar into the bowl of a free-standing mixer fitted with a dough hook, or a large mixing bowl. Mix together to combine and make a well in the centre.

Combine the butter, herbs and garlic in a food processor to form a paste. Add to the flour mix.

In a jug, mix the hot water with the milk and egg and slowly add to the dry ingredients. Mix until combined, then knead for 6 minutes in the machine or 10 minutes by hand.

Cover with oiled cling film and leave to prove for at least 90 minutes or until doubled in size.

Turn out onto a lightly floured work surface and knead for 30 seconds to knock back the dough. Divide the dough into 14–18 pieces and roll into balls.

Mix the two grated cheeses together and set aside one third. Make an indent in each of the dough balls, divide the cheese between them then seal up the dough. Place the balls on the two prepared trays: start with the middle rolls and build around them.

Loosely cover with oiled cling film and leave to prove again for 1 hour.

Preheat the oven to 200°C/400°F/Gas Mark 6.

Brush the rolls with egg wash, sprinkle over the remaining grated cheese, and bake in the oven for 18–22 minutes until golden.

CORNBREAD

When the boys were young we took them to the States. While we were there, we went to a Wild West show – you know, the one with horses and cowboys and where you get a plastic hat in the colour of the team you need to cheer for and, of course, the terrible tray of greasy chicken and ribs. Well, along with that we had some cornbread. It was so yummy I had to make it when I got home.

100g unsalted butter
3 large eggs
160ml full-fat milk
1 tbsp lemon juice
100g tinned sweetcorn, drained
170g strong white bread flour
140g polenta (cornmeal)
60g caster sugar
large pinch of sea salt
1 tsp baking powder

You will also need a 900g (2lb) loaf tin, greased and lined with baking parchment

Preheat the oven to 170°C/325°F/Gas Mark 3.

Melt the butter, pour into a large mixing bowl and allow to cool slightly. Add the eggs, milk, lemon juice, drained sweetcorn and mix to combine.

In another large bowl, sift together the strong bread flour, polenta, sugar, salt and baking powder. Make a well in the centre and gently fold in the liquid. Be careful not to overwork the mix or it will become tough once cooked.

Spoon the mixture into the prepared loaf tin. Bake straight away in the preheated oven for 40 minutes or until a skewer inserted into the middle of the cornbread comes out clean.

Carefully run a palette knife around the edges to loosen the loaf from the tin, then leave to cool in the tin for 5 minutes. Turn out onto a wire rack and leave to cool before slicing.

POTATO BREAD

A real carb fest, try this great bread. I truly love it. The potato helps to hold moisture in the dough, so you get a tasty bread that stays softer for longer – not that this hangs around for very long at my house!

**250g potatoes (Maris
  Pipers work well),
  peeled and quartered**
250g self-raising flour
½ tsp bicarbonate of soda
40g unsalted butter, melted
olive oil

**You will also need a flat
(smooth) griddle pan and a
large, solid-based frying pan**

TOP TIP
Add 1 tsp of dried rosemary
when adding the rest of the
dried ingredients to give
these easy potato breads
a delicious twist.

Put the potatoes in a large pan of water and bring to the boil, then turn down the heat and simmer for about 15 minutes or until tender. Drain the potatoes in a colander and mash until smooth. Allow to cool slightly, then transfer to a large bowl, add the self-raising flour, bicarbonate of soda and butter and stir until well combined.

Divide the dough in half. Roll out each portion into a circle the size of a dinner plate and cut into 6 triangles.

Heat the griddle, brush each triangle with olive oil and cook for 3-5 minutes on each side until golden brown.

PARMESAN AND PESTO FANTAIL LOAF

These are a reminder of Holly and Jae, who were my fellow contestants on Bake Off. *Jae made fantail rolls and since then I've wanted to try something similar. Holly, well, she is the pesto queen and my friend.*

300g strong white bread flour,
  plus extra for kneading
6g sea salt
7g easy-blend/fast-action yeast
5g caster sugar
1 tbsp olive oil
180ml lukewarm water
3–4 tbsp red or green pesto
30g Parmesan, grated

You will also need a 900g (2lb) loaf tin, greased and lined with baking parchment

Mix together the dry ingredients in a free-standing mixer fitted with a dough hook, or a large bowl, and make a well in the centre.

Add the olive oil to the water, mix together, then add to the dry ingredients; mix until combined. Knead for 6 minutes in the machine or 10 minutes by hand until the dough is smooth and elastic.

Cover the dough with oiled cling film and leave to prove for 1 hour or until doubled in size.

Tip out onto the work surface and knead for 30 seconds to knock back the dough.

Divide into 12 portions, then roll each out into 6 x 9cm tiles. Spread each tile with pesto and position the slices vertically in the prepared tin. It will look small but double in size. Cover loosely with cling film and leave to prove for 90 minutes.

Preheat the oven to 220°C/425°F/Gas Mark 7.

Sprinkle the Parmesan on top of the loaf and bake in the oven for 25–35 minutes.

Carefully run a palette knife around the edges to loosen the loaf from the tin, then leave to cool in the tin for 5 minutes. Turn out onto a wire rack and leave to cool before slicing.

PRETZELS

*Every time I go past one of those pretzel sellers in a shopping centre
I have to stop. My mouth waters and I think I'll just have the taster
piece, but I always end up buying a whole one!*

200g plain flour

300g strong white bread flour,
   plus extra for kneading

9g sea salt

7g easy-blend/fast-action yeast

10g soft brown sugar

40g unsalted butter, melted

200ml warm water

170ml full-fat milk, warmed

a large bowl of boiling water

2 tbsp baking powder

1 egg, beaten

Topping

2 tbsp ground ground cinnamon

80g caster sugar

100g unsalted butter, melted

**You will also need 2 baking
trays, greased and lined
with baking parchment**

Bits
& Bobs

Savoury pretzels
See page 248 for my trick to
making a tasty savoury version.

Tip the dry ingredients into a free-standing mixer
fitted with a dough hook, or a large mixing bowl.
Mix until combined and make a well in the centre.

In a jug, mix together the butter, warm water and
milk. Slowly add the liquid to the dry ingredients
and knead for 8 minutes in the machine or 12
minutes by hand.

Shape the dough into a ball, place in a large clean
bowl, cover with oiled cling film and leave to prove
for 90 minutes or until doubled in size.

Turn out onto a lightly floured work surface and
knead for 30 seconds to knock back the dough.

Preheat the oven to 210°C/410°F/Gas Mark 6.

Divide the dough into 14 equal pieces and roll
each into a long sausage; shape into a traditional
pretzel shape.

Pour the boiling water into a mixing bowl and
whisk in the baking powder. Using a slotted spoon,
dip each pretzel into the water bath and, still using
the slotted spoon, drain on to a clean tea towel
or piece of kitchen towel. Transfer the pretzels
to the prepared baking sheets. Leave to rest for
10 minutes and then brush with the beaten egg.

Place in the centre of the preheated oven and
bake for 8–10 minutes until golden.

Let the pretzels cool on a wire rack for 5 minutes.
Meanwhile, combine the cinnamon and sugar
together. Brush the slightly cooled pretzels with
the melted butter and sprinkle over the spiced sugar.

BLACK OLIVE AND PARMA HAM SCONES

As a thank you to all the people who worked on my first book, I hosted an afternoon tea in the garden. I tried these scones out on them and I have to say they disappeared pretty quickly.

225g self-raising flour
1 tsp cream of tartar
½ tsp bicarbonate of soda
pinch of salt
50g unsalted butter,
    diced and chilled
10 small black olives,
    each cut into 4 slices
130–150ml full-fat milk
plain flour for dusting
1 egg yolk, beaten
6 slices of Parma ham, halved

You will also need a baking
sheet lined with baking
parchment and a 5cm
plain round cutter

Preheat the oven to 220°C/425°F/Gas Mark 7.

Sift the flour, cream of tartar, bicarbonate of soda and a pinch of salt into a large mixing bowl. Add the chilled butter and using your fingers rub into the flour until the mixture resembles fine sand.

Add the olives and stir to combine. Slowly add enough milk to bring the dough together, using a table knife to do so. Turn the dough out onto a lightly floured work surface and knead very gently for 20 seconds, just enough to bring the dough together. Don't overwork the dough as this will make the scones heavy.

Roll the dough out to a thickness of 2–3cm and use the cutter to stamp out rounds. Gather any offcuts into a ball, roll out again and stamp out more scones. Place on the lined baking sheet, lightly brush the top of each scone with the beaten egg and top with a twist of Parma ham.

Bake on the middle shelf of the preheated oven for 12–14 minutes until well risen and golden.

Cool the scones on a wire rack and serve slightly warm or at room temperature.

Chapter three

CAKES

Oh how I love a nice cake! It can be a simple vanilla sponge, but when it's made well, light as a feather but buttery and unctuous, you just can't beat it. Always remember when using a free-standing mixer that owing to the electric motor having more power than a human one, you don't need to spend as long combining ingredients, so keep an eye on things to make sure you don't over mix, as this will make the texture of the cake hard. If you do a lot of baking then it will make life a lot easier to invest in a free-standing mixer.

APPLE CAKE

An old-fashioned apple cake is my sort of cake: gently spiced, dotted with sultanas and with some lovely, crunchy demerara sugar on top. If you don't like sultanas, replace them with extra diced apple.

250g unsalted butter, softened
200g caster sugar
50g ground almonds
3 large eggs
1 tsp ground cinnamon
250g plain flour
1 tsp baking powder
250g peeled and diced
    eating apples
60g sultanas
30g demerara sugar

You will also need a 23cm
springform or loose-bottomed
cake tin, greased and lined
with baking parchment

Preheat the oven to 170°C/325°F/Gas Mark 3.

Cream the butter and sugar together in a free-standing mixer or by hand wih a wooden spoon in a large mixing bowl until light and fluffy. Add the ground almonds and stir to combine.

Beat the eggs together in a jug and add gradually to the batter, beating inbetween additions as you go. If the mixture begins to curdle, add 1 tbsp of the flour.

Using a large metal spoon, carefully fold in the cinnamon, flour and baking powder, then fold in the diced apples and sultanas until completely combined.

Spoon into the prepared tin and spread level using a palette knife. Sprinkle over the demerara sugar and bake in the preheated oven for 55–65 minutes until a skewer comes out clean when inserted into the middle of the cake. Keep an eye on the cake and if it looks like it is starting to brown too quickly, cover loosely with foil.

Remove from the oven and leave to cool in the tin for at least half an hour before carefully turning out onto a wire rack to cool completely.

MINI ORANGE AND ALMOND FRIANDS

I just love the flavour of the orange blossom running through the icing glaze in these moist little mouthfuls of pleasure!

5 large egg whites
190g self-raising flour
150g icing sugar
1 tsp baking powder
120g ground almonds
200g unsalted butter,
   melted and cooled slightly
finely grated zest of 2 oranges

Icing
100g icing sugar
juice of ½ small orange
1 tsp orange blossom
   water (optional)

You will also need a 12-hole friand or muffin tin, greased with cake-release spray or a flavourless cooking oil such as sunflower or rapeseed

Preheat the oven to 170°C/325°F/Gas Mark 3.

Whisk the egg whites to soft peaks in a free-standing mixer or with an electric whisk in a large mixing bowl.

Sift the flour, icing sugar, baking powder and ground almonds together in a separate bowl. Add the dry ingredients to the beaten egg whites, folding them in carefully to avoid knocking out too much air. Fold in the melted butter and orange zest until combined.

Half fill the prepared tin and bake in the preheated oven for 20–22 minutes until golden.

Cool in the tins for 3–4 minutes and then turn out onto a wire cooling rack.

Meanwhile, make the icing by whisking the icing sugar, orange juice and orange blossom water, if using, together to make a thick but drizzly icing.

While the friands are still just warm, spoon the icing over the top half of each cake allowing it to drizzle down the sides. Leave until set before serving.

MOCHA CAKE

*A grown-up cake, decadent and tall. A little gold leaf gives it that special look.
It might seem odd to spoon mayonnaise into your cake mixture, but the result
is deliciously light and moist.*

225g margarine or unsalted
  butter, softened
200g golden caster sugar
4 large eggs
225g self-raising flour
1 shot of espresso plus ½ tsp
  instant coffee granules
  (or 2 tsp instant coffee
  granules dissolved in
  2 tbsp hot water)
30g cocoa powder
1 heaped tbsp mayonnaise

Ganache
200ml double cream
150g good-quality dark
  chocolate, roughly chopped
50g milk chocolate, roughly
  chopped

Buttercream
80g unsalted butter, softened
200g icing sugar
shot of espresso
  (or 2 tsp instant coffee
  granules dissolved in
  1 tbsp hot water)

100g dark chocolate shavings
edible gold leaf (optional)

**You will also need three 18cm
sandwich tins, lightly greased,
and a piping bag fitted with
a plain nozzle**

Preheat the oven to 170°C/325°F/Gas Mark 3.

Either in the bowl of a free-standing mixer or by hand in a large mixing bowl, cream the butter and sugar together until light and fluffy. Beat the eggs together with a fork, then add slowly to the butter mix. If it starts to curdle, add 1 tbsp of the flour to stabilise the mix. Using a large metal spoon, fold in the flour until just combined.

Spoon a third of the batter into a separate bowl and mix in the coffee. Fold the cocoa and mayonnaise into the remaining two thirds until fully incorporated.

Spoon the coffee batter into the first prepared tin and then divide the chocolate batter between the remaining two tins and bake in the middle of the preheated oven for 22–25 minutes or until a skewer comes out clean when inserted into the middle of the cakes. Turn the cakes out of the tins onto a wire cooling rack and leave until completely cold.

While the cakes are baking, make the ganache. Bring the cream to the boil in a small saucepan, then remove from the heat. Add both the dark and milk chocolate and stir until melted, smooth and shiny; chill until cold but not firm. Whisk until light, fluffy and pale and spoon into a piping bag.

To make the buttercream, beat the butter, icing sugar and coffee together in a freestanding mixer until light and fluffy.

To assemble the cake, place one of the chocolate cakes on the serving plate and pipe small rounds of the whipped ganache across the surface. Layer with the coffee sponge and repeat the process. Top with the final chocolate sponge and smooth over a generous layer of the coffee buttercream. Decorate with chocolate shavings and gold leaf if using.

BANANA, PECAN AND BUTTERSCOTCH CAKE

The flavours of pecan and toffee work so well together: turn them into pecan brittle and you have a winner on many levels. You get the sweet and salty and the soft and crunchy. This is a cake where opposites really do attract.

250g unsalted butter, softened
200g soft light brown sugar
3 large eggs, beaten
2 ripe bananas, mashed with a fork
300g self-raising flour
1 tsp ground cinnamon
1 tsp baking powder

Brittle
100g caster sugar
1 tsp white wine vinegar
12 pecan halves

Buttercream
250g unsalted butter, softened
500g icing sugar
3 tbsp dulce de leche (or homemade butterscotch, see pages 248)
1 tsp ground cinnamon

You will also need two 20cm sandwich tins, greased and lined with baking parchment, and a silicone mat or a tray lined with non-stick baking parchment paper

Preheat the oven 170°C/325°F/Gas Mark 3.

Cream the butter and sugar together until pale, light and fluffy: this is easiest in a free-standing mixer or by using an electric hand whisk. Add the eggs, one at a time, mixing well after each addition, then stir in the mashed bananas.

Using a large metal spoon, carefully fold in the flour, cinnamon and baking powder until combined. Divide the batter equally between the two prepared tins and spread level using a palette knife. Bake on the middle shelf of the preheated oven for 35-45 minutes or until golden and a skewer comes out clean when inserted into the middle of the cake. If the cakes begin to brown too quickly, cover loosely with foil.

Remove from the oven and leave to cool in the tin for 10 minutes, before carefully transferring to a wire rack to cool completely.

Meanwhile, make the brittle. Gently melt the sugar and vinegar in a saucepan over a low heat until it dissolves. Bring to the boil until the sugar turns a deep caramel colour, then remove from the heat. Using tongs, carefully dip each pecan into the caramel until completely covered, then leave to set on the silicone mat or lined tray. Leave to cool.

To make the frosting, beat the butter in a free-standing mixer or by hand in a large bowl until smooth. Gradually add the icing sugar, dulce de leche (or butterscotch) and cinnamon and beat slowly to combine.

Once the cakes have cooled, spoon half the buttercream over the first sponge and sandwich with the second. Cover the top and sides with the remaining buttercream and decorate with the individual pecan brittles.

Bits
& Bobs

Butterscotch
See page 248 to find out how
to make your own butterscotch.

Cakes

LEMON BUNDT CAKE

*This is a simple cake, finished with a yoghurt and zingy lemon icing.
If you don't have a bundt tin, you can use any doughnut-shaped tin. Because
of the high sugar content it will have a darker crust, so do keep an eye on it,
but don't worry – the sponge will still be lovely and soft on the inside.*

250g unsalted butter, softened
300g caster sugar
finely grated zest of 2 lemons
4 large eggs
100ml lemon juice
100ml double cream
440g self-raising flour
1 tsp baking powder
100g lemon curd

Icing
200g icing sugar
2 tbsp natural yoghurt
1 tbsp lemon curd

**You will also need a bundt tin,
greased with cake-release spray
or a flavourless cooking oil such
as sunflower or rapeseed**

Preheat the oven to 170°C/325°F/Gas Mark 3.

Either in the bowl of a free-standing mixer
or by hand with an electric hand whisk, in a
large mixing bowl, cream the butter, sugar and
lemon zest together until light and fluffy. Beat
the eggs together in a jug then gradually add
to the creamed butter, mixing well between
each addition.

Mix together 1 tbsp of the lemon juice with the
cream to thicken it, then add to the bowl along
with the remaining lemon juice, using a large
metal spoon to combine. Carefully fold in the
flour and baking powder.

Spoon half the mixture into the prepared tin.
Spoon or pipe the lemon curd in an even layer over
the top of this, then spoon over the remaining cake
batter. Bake on the middle shelf of the preheated
oven for 55–70 minutes until golden and a skewer
inserted into the cake comes out clean. If you
notice the cake browning too quickly, cover
loosely with foil.

Remove from the oven and leave to cool in the
tin for 10 minutes,then carefully turn out onto
a wire rack to cool completely.

Meanwhile, mix the icing sugar, yoghurt and
lemon curd together to make a thick paste.
While the icing is still wet, spread over the cake.
Leave the icing to set before serving.

LIME AND COCONUT TRAY BAKE

The combined flavour of lime and coconut is sublime. The pairing of these two ingredients makes for a cake that is a little less sweet than normal, but with the icing and desiccated coconut on top, it works so well.

320g margarine or unsalted butter, softened
270g caster sugar
320g self-raising flour
5 large eggs
finely grated zest of 2 limes
50g desiccated coconut

Topping
75ml water
100g caster sugar
200g icing sugar
finely grated zest and juice of 2-4 limes
50g desiccated coconut
crystallized lime (optional)

You will also need a 20 x 30cm baking tin, greased and lined with baking parchment

Bits & Bobs

Cheat's crystallised citrus fruits
These give a lovely texture and are very pretty to sprinkle on to any cake. See page 248 for my recipe.

Preheat the oven to 170°C/325°F/Gas Mark 3.

Tip all of the cake ingredients (except the lime juice) into the bowl of a free-standing mixer and beat for 2 minutes until smooth.

Pour the cake batter into the prepared tin and spread level using a palette knife.

Bake on the middle shelf of the preheated oven for about 50-60 minutes or until well risen, golden and a skewer inserted into the middle of the cake comes out clean.

Meanwhile, make a lime syrup by bringing the water and caster sugar to the boil in a saucepan. Reduce the heat and let the syrup simmer until thickened and reduced by half; it should be the consistency to coat the back of a spoon. Add half the juice and zest and stir to combine. Remove from the heat.

Remove the cake from the oven and pierce the top of the cake all over with a wooden skewer. Slowly drizzle over the syrup while the cake is still warm and in the tin but be careful not to flood it.

Make the icing by combining 3 tbsp of the remaining lime juice with the icing sugar. Set aside.

Toast the desiccated coconut in a dry frying pan over a low-medium heat until the coconut turns golden – this will happen quickly, so don't leave the pan unattended!

Remove the cake from the tin, pour over the icing and top with the toasted coconut and remaining lime zest (or crystallised lime if using) Leave to set for half an hour and then slice into squares.

CHOCOLATE AND PEAR TORTE

A chocolate and pear perfection, this is a great dessert cake, fantastic for wheat-intolerant friends. Serve with warm chocolate sauce and dessert wine.

250ml water

60g caster sugar

peel of half an orange

3 small dessert pears, peeled, cored and quartered

300g good-quality dark chocolate, roughly chopped

250g unsalted butter

4 large eggs, separated

100g caster sugar

200g ground almonds

pinch of sea salt

1 tsp vanilla extract or vanilla bean paste

You will also need a 25cm springform or loose-bottomed cake tin, lightly greased

Bits & Bobs

Poached pear dessert
See page 248 for my recipe for a xx dessert.

Preheat the oven to 170°C/325°F/Gas Mark 3.

Put the water, caster sugar and orange peel in a saucepan and bring to the boil, stirring to dissolve the sugar. Add the pears, cover the pan with a lid and simmer for 5-10 minutes until just softened (the time this takes will depend on the ripeness of the pears). Remove the pears using a slotted spoon and leave to cool. Continue to cook the poaching liquid until reduced by half and thick and syrupy; set aside.

Melt the chocolate and butter together in a heatproof bowl over a pan of barely simmering water. Stir until smooth and remove from the heat.

Whisk the egg whites until they reach a stiff peak. In a separate bowl, whisk the yolks and sugar together until pale, light and fluffy. Using a metal spoon and being careful not to knock out any of the air, fold in the almonds, salt and vanilla into the egg yolk mixture. Add a spoonful of the egg white and beat in to loosen the mixture, before carefully folding in the remaining whites. Finally, fold in the melted chocolate and butter.

Pour the mixture into the prepared tins and push the quartered pears into the batter in a circular shape. Bake on the middle shelf of the preheated oven for 25–35 minutes until the torte begins to come away from the sides of the tin.

Run a palette knife around the sides of the tin and remove the ring from the tin but not the base, and leave the torte to cool completely on a rack. Chill for a minimum of 2 hours, then carefully slide the torte off the base onto a plate. Brush with the reduced pear syrup to serve.

HONEY MADELEINES

A few years ago I was lucky enough to be taken to dinner in Daniel Boulud's restaurant in New York. We had the most amazing dinner but what stuck in my mind were the madeleines: they were warm, soft and buttery with a dusting of icing sugar. This is my take on Daniel's recipe. Serve with a pot of warm honey.

100g self raising flour
1 tsp baking powder
pinch of sea salt
2 large eggs
50g caster sugar
4 tbsp honey
90g unsalted butter, melted
icing sugar for dusting

You will also need a madeleine pan, greased with cake release spray or a flavourless vegetable oil such as sunflower or rapeseed, plus a piping bag. You can find the pans in most good homeware stores or online

Sift the flour, baking powder and salt into a large mixing bowl.

In another bowl, or using a free-standing mixer, whisk together the eggs, sugar and 2 tsbps honey until pale and frothy. Add the sieved dry ingredients and whisk until just combined.

Stir in the melted butter, cover with cling film and chill for at least 1 hour.

Preheat the oven to 200°C/400°F/Gas Mark 6.

Pour the batter into a piping bag, snip about 1cm off the bottom and pipe the moulds in the madeleine pan two-thirds full. Bake for 5 minutes, reduce the oven to 180°C/350°F/Gas Mark 4, and rotate the madeleine tin in the oven. Bake for a further 5 minutes until the centres of the cakes rise and the edges are golden brown.

Remove from the oven and serve the madeleines warm, brushed with the remaining honey.

VICTORIA SPONGE

When I was writing A Passion for Baking, *my friend Michelle was very disappointed that I didn't mention her. My Victoria sponge is her favourite so this one is for you, my lovely friend.*

200g self-raising flour
1 tsp baking powder
200g caster sugar
200g margarine
4 large eggs, beaten
1 large egg yolk
1 tsp vanilla extract
   or vanilla bean paste

Filling
4 tbsp raspberry jam
2 tbsp caster sugar, to serve

You will also need two 20cm sandwich tins, greased and lined with a disc of buttered baking parchment

Preheat the oven to 180°C/350°F/Gas Mark 4.

Tip all the cake ingredients into the bowl of a free-standing mixer and beat for 1–2 minutes until smooth. If you don't have a mixer, you can use an electric hand-held mixer.

Divide the batter evenly between the prepared cake tins and spread level using a palette knife. Bake on the middle shelf of the preheated oven for 25–30 minutes until golden, well risen and a skewer inserted into the middle of the cakes comes out clean.

Remove from the oven and carefully turn the cakes out of the tins. Peel off the parchment and turn the cakes the right way up. Leave to cool on wire cooling racks.

Place one of the cooled cakes on a serving plate or cake stand, right side up, and spread with the jam. Top with the second cake and sprinkle with caster sugar to serve.

RASPBERRY GENOISE LAYER CAKE

This looks and sounds impressive but doesn't really take much more effort than a normal sponge. The key is to get all your ingredients ready in advance so that once you've beaten the eggs you can get the cake into the oven.

6 large eggs
200g caster sugar
80g unsalted butter, melted
1 tsp vanilla extract or
  vanilla bean paste
200g plain flour
2 tbsp raspberry liqueur
  such as Chambord

Filling
600ml double cream
3–4 tbsp raspberry jam
600g raspberries
1 tbsp caster sugar
½ tsp raspberry liqueur
  such as Chambord
50g white chocolate bar
  (optional)

You will also need three 20cm sandwich tins, greased and lined with baking parchment

Bits
& Bobs

White chocolate shavings
These make a lovely (and easy!) garnish
for cake. You can make them with a
vegetable peeler by pulling it towards
you over a bar of chocolate. Just make
sure the chocolate is room temperature.

Preheat the oven to 180°C/350°F/Gas Mark 4.

Break the eggs into a heatproof bowl, add the sugar and place over a pan of simmering water. Beat with an electric whisk until the mixture has doubled in volume and leaves a ribbon trail on the surface when you remove the whisk.

Combine the melted butter and vanilla extract and fold into the mix using a metal spoon. Sift in the flour and gently fold in until combined. Divide the batter equally between the 3 cake tins and bake in the preheated oven, just above the middle shelf, for 25 minutes until golden and a skewer comes out clean when inserted into the middle of the cake.

Remove from the oven and leave to cool in the tins. Once completely cool, remove the cakes from the tins and brush with the raspberry liqueur.

Meanwhile, to make the filling, whisk 400ml of the cream until it forms soft peaks. Fold in the jam and half of the raspberries.

Place the first sponge on a cake stand and spread with half the raspberry cream. Place the second sponge on top and repeat the process; top with the third and final sponge.

Whisk the remaining 200ml of double cream until soft peaks form and spread on the top of the cake. Toss the remaining raspberries, the caster sugar and half a teaspoon of raspberry liqueur gently to combine, then arrange in a pretty crowning layer, pointy sides up, over the top.

STEM GINGER CHEESECAKE

A good cheesecake is my sign of a good pastry chef: it has to be creamy but not wet and the base crisp but never too thick. Once you have one you like, you can adapt it and make it your own. I'm really hoping this will be the one.

70g unsalted butter

15-20 ginger nut biscuits

600g full-fat cream cheese

2 tbsp plain flour

175g caster sugar, plus 1tbsp

2 tsp vanilla extract
    or vanilla bean paste

2 large eggs

1 large egg yolk

142ml sour cream (see Top
    Tip page 220) plus 3 tbsps

5 nuggets stem ginger in
    syrup plus extra to serve

You will also need a 20cm springform cake tin, lightly greased, and a baking tray

Bits
& Bobs

Chocolate ganache
For a grown-up take on this spicy cheesecake, add a layer of dark chocolate ganache – the two flavours work perfectly together. See page 248 for my recipe.

Preheat the oven to 170°C/325°F/Gas Mark 3.

Melt the butter in a small pan or in the microwave on a low setting in 10-second bursts. Crush the biscuits in a food processor, or in a sandwich bag with a rolling pin until they are fine crumbs, and tip into a bowl. Add the melted butter and mix to thoroughly combine.

Press the buttery crumbs into the base of the cake tin in an even layer and bake on a baking tray on the middle shelf of the preheated oven for 5 minutes. Remove from the oven and allow to cool while you prepare the filling.

Beat the cream cheese until smooth, then add the flour, 175g sugar, vanilla, eggs, yolk and the 142ml sour cream and beat again until smooth, light and fluffy.

Drain the ginger from the jar, reserving the syrup for later. Finely dice and mix into the batter until thoroughly combined. Carefully pour into the cake tin on top of the biscuit base, and spread level using a palette knife.

Place on a baking tray and bake on the middle shelf of the oven for 30–35 minutes until just set.

Mix together the remaining caster sugar and sour cream and carefully spoon onto the top of the baked cheesecake . Return to the oven for a further 3-4 minutes until just set.

Remove from the oven and let the cheesecake cool in the tin. Chill in the tin in the fridge for at least 4 hours or overnight until ready to serve. Drizzle over the reserved stem ginger syrup and scatter with more chopped ginger if you like.

ULTIMATE CHOCOLATE CAKE

Every baking book needs 'that' chocolate cake, the one you can pull out of the bag and know that it will impress, comfort and celebrate – and this is the one. This cake looks amazing and tastes even better, and you can decorate it with whatever takes your fancy.

175g unsalted butter, softened

300g caster sugar

3 large eggs, beaten

75g self-raising flour

200g plain flour

1 tsp bicarbonate of soda

75g cocoa powder

200ml sour cream, at room
  temperature (see Top
  Tip page 220)

50g full-fat cream cheese,
  at room temperature

100g white chocolate,
  roughly chopped

Decoration

300g double cream

150g good-quality dark
  chocolate, finely chopped

150g milk chocolate,
  finely chopped

16-24 Cadbury Dairy Milk
  'Little Bars'

chocolate truffles, sweets
  or fresh soft fruits (such
  as raspberries, strawberries)

Preheat the oven to 180°C/350°F/Gas Mark 4.

Beat the butter and caster sugar together until pale, light and fluffy: this is easiest using a free-standing mixer or an electric hand-held mixer.

Add the beaten eggs a little at a time, beating well between each addition.

Sift both flours, the bicarbonate of soda and the cocoa into a large bowl. Add half the sifted dry ingredients to the butter-and-egg mixture and fold in using a large metal spoon.

In another bowl, mix together the sour cream and cream cheese until smooth and fold half into the cake mixture. Repeat this process with the remaining flour and sour cream and mix until smooth.

Fold the chopped white chocolate and spoon the cake batter into the prepared tin. Spread level using a palette knife.

Bake on the middle shelf of the preheated oven for about 1 hour or until a skewer inserted into the middle of the cake comes out clean.

You will also need a 20cm springform cake tin, buttered and the base lined with a disc of buttered baking parchment, and a wide ribbon

TOP TIP
If you need to make the chocolate bars the right height in proportion to your cake, use them at room temperature and trim them down (this works particularly well with Milky Bars). This will also give the cake a more informal look.

Leave the cake to cool in the tin for 10 minutes before turning out onto a wire rack.

Meanwhile, prepare your decoration. Make a chocolate ganache by bringing the cream to the boil in a pan. Remove from the heat, then add the chopped chocolates and stir until smooth and shiny. Allow to cool completely.

Spread a thin layer of the ganache over the sides and top of the cake using a palette knife. Stick the chocolate bars around the cake, with the smooth sides facing out. Wrap with a thick ribbon to keep the bars in place.

Fill the centre of the cake with your favourite sweets, chocolate truffles or soft fruits.

UPSIDE-DOWN PINEAPPLE CAKE

*This is another childhood favourite of mine. I've upped the ante with
a mint sugar syrup and a splash of rum – it's like a mojito in a cake!
If you're not a fan of rum, you can replace it with milk.*

**225g margarine or unsalted
   butter, softened**
175g soft light brown sugar
3 large eggs, beaten
**1 tbsp white or dark rum
   (or milk)**
250g self-raising flour
**432g tinned pineapple rings
   (in juice)**
8 firm raspberries

Mint syrup
50g caster sugar
handful of fresh mint

**You will also need a 20cm
springform or loose-bottomed
cake tin, lightly greased and
lined with baking parchment**

Preheat the oven to 170°C/325°F/Gas Mark 3.

Cream together the margarine or butter and sugar
in a free-standing mixer or by hand in a large bowl
until light and fluffy.

In a separate bowl, combine the eggs with the rum or
milk, then add gradually to the butter and sugar mix,
stirring well between each addition until combined.
Using a large metal spoon, fold in the flour.

Drain the pineapple (reserving the liquid). Line the
bottom of the prepared tin with the pineapple rings
(7-8 should fit snuggly). Place a raspberry (pointy side
facing down) in the centre of each ring. Spoon over
the cake batter and spread level using a palette knife.

Bake in the preheated oven on the middle shelf for
45 minutes or until golden and a skewer comes out
clean when inserted in the middle of the cake.

Run a palette knife around the edge of the cake. Place
a plate and turn the cake over and out of the tin and
onto the plate. Remove the tin and parchment.

Make the mint sugar syrup. Crush together the sugar
and mint in a pestle and mortar, or use a bowl and the
end of a rolling pin, and add to a small saucepan with
the reserved pineapple juice. Bring to the boil and
simmer for 5 minutes until thick and syrupy. Leave
to cool slightly, before straining and painting over
the baked cake as a glaze.

LEMON, WHITE CHOCOLATE AND MACADAMIA BOMBS

These are a little tricky but worth the extra effort. Give yourself plenty of time and clear a space in your freezer in advance. I promise at the end of it you'll have a real show-stopper. For a step-by-step guide, have a look at the mini chocolate, coffee and walnut cakes on my blog, Jo's Blue AGA.

Cake
125g self-raising flour
125g margarine or unsalted butter, softened
100g caster sugar
finely grated zest of 1 lemon
2 large eggs

Biscuits
35g flour plus extra for dusting
25g unsalted butter
15g macadamia nuts
15g caster sugar

Buttercream
75g butter, softened
finely grated zest of 1 lemon
125g icing sugar

Preheat the oven to 170°C/325°F/Gas Mark 3.

Tip all the cake ingredients into the bowl of a food processor and mix for 1 minute until smooth. Pour into the prepared tin and spread level using a palette knife. Bake for 15–18 minutes until golden and a skewer comes out clean when inserted into the centre of the cake. Turn out onto a wire rack and cool completely, before cutting into 12 rounds using the cutters.

Meanwhile, blend the biscuit ingredients together in a food processor, turn out onto a lightly floured work surface and, using your hands, form the crumbs into a dough. Roll out the dough to a thickness of around 2mm and stamp out 6–8 biscuits using the cutters. Arrange on the lined baking tray and chill for 30 minutes until firm. Bake in the preheated oven for 12–15 minutes until just golden. Leave to cool on the tray for 5 minutes before transferring onto a wire cooling rack.

Next, make the buttercream by creaming the butter and lemon zest in the food processor until smooth. Gradually incorporate the icing sugar on a slow speed until the mixture is soft and light.

Topping
**300g white chocolate,
roughly chopped**
**20g macadamia nuts,
crushed**
or lemon zest

**You will also need a small
20 x 28cm Swiss roll tin,
greased and lined with
baking parchment, a 5cm
ring cutter, a baking tray
lined with parchment
paper, and a piping bag.**

When you are ready to assemble, place the biscuits on the baking tray. Fill the piping bag with the buttercream, snip about 1 ½ cms off the end of the bag and pipe an even layer over them. Top with a disc of sponge, then another layer of piped buttercream; repeat the process so that you have 1 layer of biscuit, 3 of buttercream and 2 of sponge. Transfer to the freezer and chill for half an hour or until solid.

Melt the white chocolate in a heatproof bowl over a pan of simmering water. If using a microwave melt the chocolate in 10-second bursts on a low setting. Stir until smooth and remove from the heat.

Transfer the frozen stacks to a wire cooling rack and pour the melted chocolate over until the bombs are completely encased. Sprinkle with the crushed nuts or crystallised lemon peel (see page 248). Pop back on the lined baking tray and chill until set. Serve at room temperature.

Chapter
four

BAKING WITH CHILDREN

Anyone who knows me knows how I feel about teaching children to cook and bake. I really do believe it could be one of the most important things you can do as a parent. The saying 'We are what we eat' is so true, and giving a child an interest in food from an early age and the confidence to prepare dishes could hopefully keep them away from eating too much fast food. It's a wonderful way to spend time with your child, plus you end up with some scrummy, home-cooked food – what's not to like?!

TOFFEE CRISP CHOCOLATE BALLS

A Rice Krispies cake on a stick, covered with chocolate and sprinkles, this treat would make a perfect craft activity at a school fair. The mixture can be halved or doubled, as required.

300g milk chocolate, chopped
200g marshmallows
20g unsalted butter
100g Kellogg's Rice Krispies
sprinkles

**You will also need 20
lollipop sticks**

TOP TIP
It's a good idea to divide the chocolate between two bowls to make sure it stays Rice Krispie free when dunking.

Melt the milk chocolate either in a heatproof bowl over a pan of barely simmering water or in the microwave on a low setting in 20-second bursts. Stir until smooth and set aside.

Melt the marshmallows and butter together in a heatproof bowl in the microwave or over a low heat in a pan.

Add the Rice Krispies and stir to combine – the mixture will be sticky. Using clean hands quick roll the mixture into 20 golf ball shapes and push a lollipop stick into each one.

Tip the sprinkles out onto a plate. Dip each ball halfway into the melted chocolate and then stand them in the sprinkles so that the tops are coated. Chill until completely set.

LEMON AND WHITE CHOCOLATE MUFFINS

Muffins are great to make with children. All you need to do is measure the dry ingredients into a large mixing bowl and the wet into a jug and then give them a little stir together. This is one recipe where lumps are OK, as an overworked muffin batter will produce a heavy muffin.

280g self-raising flour
½ tsp bicarbonate of soda
½ tsp baking powder
160g caster sugar
90g unsalted butter, melted
1 large egg
finely grated zest and juice
    of 1 large (or 2 small) lemons
300ml milk
150g white chocolate bar,
    roughly chopped
1–2 tbsp demerara sugar

You will also need a
12-hole muffin tin lined
with paper cases

Preheat the oven to 180°C/350°F/Gas Mark 4

Combine the flour, bicarbonate of soda, baking powder and caster sugar in a large bowl and make a well in the centre.

In a jug, whisk together the melted butter, egg, lemon juice and zest and add the milk.

Pour the wet ingredients and chopped chocolate into the well in the dry ingredients, and fold together using a large metal spoon until just combined. Do not overwork the batter.

Divide the batter between the muffin cases and sprinkle the top of each with the demerara sugar. Bake on the middle shelf of the preheated oven for 30-35 minutes until well risen, golden brown and a skewer inserted into the middle of a muffin comes out clean.

Cool slightly on a wire rack before serving warm or at room temperature.

CHEESY MINI KETCHUP SCONES

These are perfect for little fingers and great to serve at children's birthday teas. They're easy to make and the acidity in the ketchup makes them wonderfully light and beautifully pink. Serve warm with a little unsalted butter.

225g self-raising flour
1 tsp cream of tartar
½ tsp bicarbonate of soda
pinch of sea salt
50g unsalted butter,
   diced and chilled
1 heaped tbsp tomato ketchup
50g Cheddar, grated
130–150ml full-fat milk
plain flour for dusting
1 egg, beaten with 1 tbsp milk

Toppings
1 tbsp Cheddar, grated,
   or 1 tsp sesame seeds

You will also need a 5cm plain round cutter and a baking tray lined with baking parchment

Preheat the oven to 220°C/425°F/Gas Mark 7.

Sift the flour, cream of tartar, bicarbonate of soda and salt into a large mixing bowl. Rub in the butter with the tips of your fingers until the mixture looks like fine sand.

Add the ketchup and cheese. Slowly add enough milk to bring the dough together, using a table knife to do so.

Turn out the dough onto a floured work surface and give it a little knead for about 20 seconds: don't overwork the dough, as this will make the scones heavy.

Roll out to a thickness of 2–3cm and cut into rounds using the cutter and place on the lined baking tray, in two tight rows of 5 so that they are just touching. Brush with the egg wash and sprinkle with either the grated Cheddar or sesame seeds.

Bake for 12 minutes on the middle shelf of the preheated oven, until well risen and golden.

Cool on a wire rack and serve warm.

OWL CUPCAKES

*These cute little fellows will amuse and delight all children.
I can't wait to try them out with the light of my life, my grandson Harley.*

**200g Stork or unsalted
 butter, softened**
200g caster sugar
3 large eggs, beaten
**½ tsp vanilla extract
 or vanilla bean paste**
200g self-raising flour
2 tbsp full-fat milk

Buttercream
500g icing sugar
**250g unsalted butter,
 softened**
**1 tsp vanilla extract
 or vanilla bean paste**

Decoration
120 milk chocolate buttons
24 white chocolate buttons
36 orange Smarties
gel food colouring

**You will also need a
12-hole muffin tin lined
with paper cases**

Preheat the oven to 170°C/325°F/Gas Mark 3.

In the bowl of a free-standing mixer, cream the margarine or butter and sugar together until light and fluffy.

Gradually add the beaten eggs, mixing well between each addition. Sift in the flour and mix to combine. Add the milk and vanilla and mix again until smooth.

Divide the mixture between the paper cases and bake on the middle shelf of the preheated oven for 20–25 minutes until a wooden skewer inserted into the middle of the cakes comes out clean.

Leave to cool on a wire rack until cold.

Meanwhile, make the buttercream. Beat the butter and vanilla in a free-standing mixer or by hand in a large bowl until smooth. Gradually add the icing sugar and beat on slow speed to combine.

Divide the buttercream among the 12 cupcakes and smooth flat with a palette knife. Use 2 white chocolate buttons per cake for the eyes, create wings using 10 milk chocolate buttons per cake, and divide the remainder in half to make ears.

Use the Smarties for the feet and beak of the owls and add detail with a gel food colouring.

CORN AND BACON FRITTERS

A great one for the kids to help with - a bit of a stir, then a hand from mum or dad with the frying. These are excellent served with a crispy chicken escalope.

2 tbsp olive oil
½ small onion, diced
65g diced pancetta or bacon
100g self-raising flour
100ml full-fat milk
1 large egg
20g unsalted butter, melted
30g Cheddar, grated
40g tinned sweetcorn

Heat 1 tbsp of the olive oil in a frying pan, and cook the onion and pancetta or bacon together until the onions are softened and the pancetta begins to brown. Set mixture to one side and wipe out the pan.

In a bowl, mix together the flour, milk, egg, melted butter and Cheddar until combined and smooth. Add the softened onions and cooked bacon or pancetta and stir again.

Brush the remaining olive oil in the frying pan, or use a flat hotplate, and pour in 3 ladles of the batter to make 3 small fritters. Divide half of the sweetcorn between the fritters and cook for 1–2 minutes on each side until golden. Repeat with the remaining batter and sweetcorn.

TOMMY TORTOISE LOAF

A great way to get a fussy eater to try a sandwich, my grandson Harley loves Tommy tortoise's cousin, Harley hedgehog, who appeared in my first book, A Passion for Baking.

300g strong bread flour,
    plus extra for dusting
6g sea salt
10g caster sugar
7g easy-blend/fast-action yeast
15g unsalted butter, melted
230ml full-fat milk, lukewarm
1 egg, beaten with 1 tbsp milk
1 raisin, cut in half

Tip the flour, salt, sugar and yeast either into the bowl of a free-standing mixer fitted with a dough hook or into a large bowl and mix until combined. Make a well in the middle of the dry ingredients.

Add the butter and milk to the dry ingredients and mix until combined. Knead for 6 minutes in the machine or 10 minutes by hand until smooth and soft.

Put the dough into a lightly greased mixing bowl, cover with cling film and leave to rise for 1½ hours or until doubled in size.

Turn out onto a lightly floured work surface and knead for 30 seconds to knock back the dough. Divide the dough into a quarter and a three-quarter piece. Take the three-quarter portion of the dough and shape into a neat round to create the body of the tortoise. Place in the centre of the prepared baking tray.

Take the remaining quarter of dough and cut into thirds. Use the first third to create the head, again shaping into a neat round, and position at the top of the body.

Continued overleaf

When you are shaping bread into rolls or a loaf, pull the sides down and tuck under to form a neat ball. This will help the bread rise evenly upwards rather than outwards.

With the remaining two thirds, divide each in half again, shape and position on the body for the four feet.

Pinch the bottom of the tortoise to create a small tail and leave to prove for 45–60 minutes.

Preheat the oven to 200ºC/400ºF/Gas Mark 6.

Brush the tortoise with egg wash and using a sharp kitchen knife lightly score the body into diamonds. Use the end of the knife to make a small hole for each of the eyes in the head and push in the raisin halves. Make a small, 1cm indentation for the mouth.

Bake in the middle of the preheated oven for 18–22 minutes until golden and crusty and the loaf sounds hollow when tapped underneath.

Cool on a wire rack before serving.

MUFFIN-PAN
PASTA FRITTATAS

These are great served hot as teatime treat or cold in the lunchbox or for a beach picnic as they are so quick and easy to prepare. Best of all, they use up all the leftovers. You can even use leftover spaghetti bolognese, carbonara or any leftover pasta dish – just replace the penne and chicken with 150g of pasta leftovers, snip the spaghetti into bite-sized pieces, and top with 60g grated Cheddar.

4 large eggs
2 tbsp double cream
1 heaped tbsp basil pesto
sea salt
black pepper, freshly ground
100g cooked penne pasta
100g shredded roast chicken

You will also need a 6-hole muffin pan, lightly greased with butter

Preheat the oven to 190°C/375°C/Gas Mark 5.

Beat the eggs with the double cream and pesto and season with sea salt and freshly ground black pepper.

Add the pasta and chicken and stir to combine. Divide the mixture among the muffin moulds, making sure each has an equal amount of the filling.

Bake in the preheated oven for 12–15 minutes until the muffins are just set and still have a little wobble at their centres.

Leave to rest in the pan for 2–3 minutes before turning out and serving hot or cold.

Bits
& Bobs

Grown-up frittata
See page 248 for a more grown-up
version of this frittata.

BAKED RICE PUDDING

This is so easy, your kids will barely need any supervision at all.
My boys have always loved rice pudding. It's a nursery classic at its best.

125g pudding rice
800ml full-fat milk
100ml double cream
60g caster sugar
50g unsalted butter, cubed
½ tsp freshly grated nutmeg

You will also need an
18cm round Pyrex dish
with an 8cm depth, with
a lid, and a baking tray

Bits
& Bobs

Macerated sultanas
I love to serve rice pudding with
orange-soaked sultanas. See page
248 for a delicious topping idea
for my rice pudding.

Preheat the oven to 200°C/400°F/Gas Mark 6.

Tip the rice, 700ml of the milk, the cream, sugar and butter into the dish and stir gently to combine. Place the dish, with the lid on, on a baking tray and bake in the preheated oven for 20 minutes.

Turn the oven down to 100°C/200°F/Gas Mark ½ and bake the pudding for a further 2½ hours until the rice is tender and half of the liquid has been absorbed.

Stir through the remaining milk and sprinkle over the grated nutmeg. Turn the oven up to 180°C/350°F/Gas Mark 4 and return the pudding to the oven without its lid.

Cook for a further 1 hour or until the rice is plump and tender.

SWEETIE SPECTACULAR TRAYBAKE

Cake, sweets, icing – what more can I say? You'll be the greatest. My boys' friends still talk about the chocolate version I did many years ago.

340g unsalted butter, softened
340g caster sugar
5 large eggs, beaten
340g self-raising flour
50ml full-fat milk
1 tsp vanilla extract or vanilla bean paste

Topping
400g icing sugar
200g unsalted butter, softened
2 tbsps water
400g old-fashioned sweets such as flying saucers, foam shrimps, Jelly Tots, jelly babies, jelly snakes, Smarties, lolly pops

You will also need a 30 x 23cm sandwich tin, greased and lined with baking parchment

Preheat the oven to 180°C/350°F/Gas Mark 4.

Cream the butter and caster sugar together until pale, light and fluffy in a free-standing mixer or with an electric hand-held whisk. Gradually add the beaten eggs, mixing well between each addition. Sift in the flour and mix to combine. Add the milk and vanilla, and mix again until smooth.

Spoon the mixture into the prepared tin and spread level using a palette knife.

Bake on the middle shelf of the preheated oven for 60–70 minutes until well risen, golden and springy to touch, or when a skewer inserted into the middle of the cake comes out clean. Leave to cool in the tin.

Make the butter icing by whipping the butter, icing sugar and water together in a free-standing machine or with an electric handwhisk until light and fluffy. Use a palette knife to spread the buttercream over the cooled cake. Pile on a mixture of the sweets and slice into small squares.

Chapter five

CRUMBLES, TARTS AND PITHIVIERS

*My Nan is my pastry hero. She taught me everything
I needed to know about it. From the age of three she
would stand me next to her and with patience, love
and guidance, teach me the art of good pastry making:
never handle pastry too much; let it rest; remember
to add the liquid little by little; you can always add
liquid but never take it away … these were some of
her wise words that will stand you in good stead.*

SWEETCRUST PASTRY

This pastry can be a little tricky to work with as the icing sugar tends to make it slightly softer, so don't be tempted to miss out the resting and chilling stage. It's best to roll out between two sheets of baking parchment, too, as this makes it easy to transfer to the pie dish or baking tray.

**250g plain flour, plus
extra for rolling out
125g unsalted butter,
chilled and diced
25g icing or caster sugar
pinch of sea salt
2 large egg yolks
2–3 tbsp full-fat milk**

Put the flour, butter, sugar and salt into the bowl of a food processor fitted with a metal blade.

Whizz using the pulse button until you have a breadcrumb consistency.

Add the egg yolks, whizz briefly, then add the milk a tablespoon at a time until the dough comes together.

Turn onto a lightly floured work surface and work the dough very briefly with your hands until it is smooth. Flatten into a disc and wrap in cling film and chill for at least half an hour before using.

STILTON AND BROCCOLI TART

This is a great veggie tart – the classic pairing of Stilton and broccoli really packs a punch – and the salad mentioned below complements it perfectly.

½ **quantity of shortcrust pastry (see page 132) or 200g ready-rolled shortcrust pastry**
flour for rolling out
1 egg yolk, beaten
150g broccoli
150g Stilton, broken into chunks
4 large eggs
300ml double cream
pinch of pepper

You will also need a 20cm tart tin and baking beans

Bits
& Bobs

Pear, walnut and watercress salad
See page 249 for a delicious side salad
to serve with this dish.

Preheat the oven to 190°C/375°F/Gas Mark 5.

Roll out the pastry on a lightly floured work surface, or between two sheets of baking parchment, to a thickness of a £1 coin. Carefully line the tart tin, being sure to push the pastry neatly into the corners and trimming off any excess pastry from the top. Prick the base of the tart shell several times with a fork. Screw up a sheet of baking parchment and use to line the inside of the pastry case. Chill for 10 minutes in the freezer.

Tip the baking beans into the lined pastry case and blind bake on the middle shelf of the oven for 10 minutes or until the pastry turns a pale golden colour. Remove the parchment and beans. Brush the case with the beaten yolk and return to the oven for 5 minutes.

Meanwhile, break the broccoli into 5cm florets, trimming any stalks, and steam for 3 minutes until still al dente. Evenly distribute the steamed broccoli and Stilton chunks inside the pastry case.

Beat the eggs, cream and pepper together and pour over the broccoli and cheese. Bake in the oven for 18–22 minutes until golden and just set – there should still be a slight wobble in the centre.

Leave to cool in the tin for 10 minutes, before transferring to a wire rack to cool completely.

APRICOT FRANGIPANE

Big, fat apricots in a moist almondy tart – this needs nothing more than a serving of cold single cream.

**1 quantity sweetcrust pastry
  (see page 114)**
plain flour for rolling out
240g tinned apricots, drained

Frangipane
250g unsalted butter
250g caster sugar
4 large eggs
150g self-raising flour
100g ground almonds

**You will also need a 23cm
tart tin with a depth of about
3–5cm and baking beans**

Preheat the oven to 180°C/350°F/Gas Mark 4.

Lightly dust the work surface with flour and roll the chilled pastry out into a neat disc with a thickness of about 2mm. Carefully line the tart tin, pushing the pastry neatly into the corners and trimming off the excess from the top. Prick the base of the tart shell several times with a fork. Screw up a sheet of baking parchment and use to line the inside of the pastry case. Chill for 10 minutes in the freezer.

Tip the baking beans into the lined pastry case and blind bake on the middle shelf of the oven for 18–20 minutes until the pastry turns a pale golden colour. Remove the parchment and beans.

To make the filling, beat together the butter, sugar, eggs, flour and ground almonds until light and fluffy. Spoon the frangipane into the pastry case and spread level. Arrange the apricot halves evenly spaced, rounded side uppermost in the frangipane. Bake for 50–60 minutes until golden. If the tart starts to brown too quickly, cover the top loosely with foil.

Leave to cool in the tin for 10 minutes, then transfer to a wire rack to cool completely.

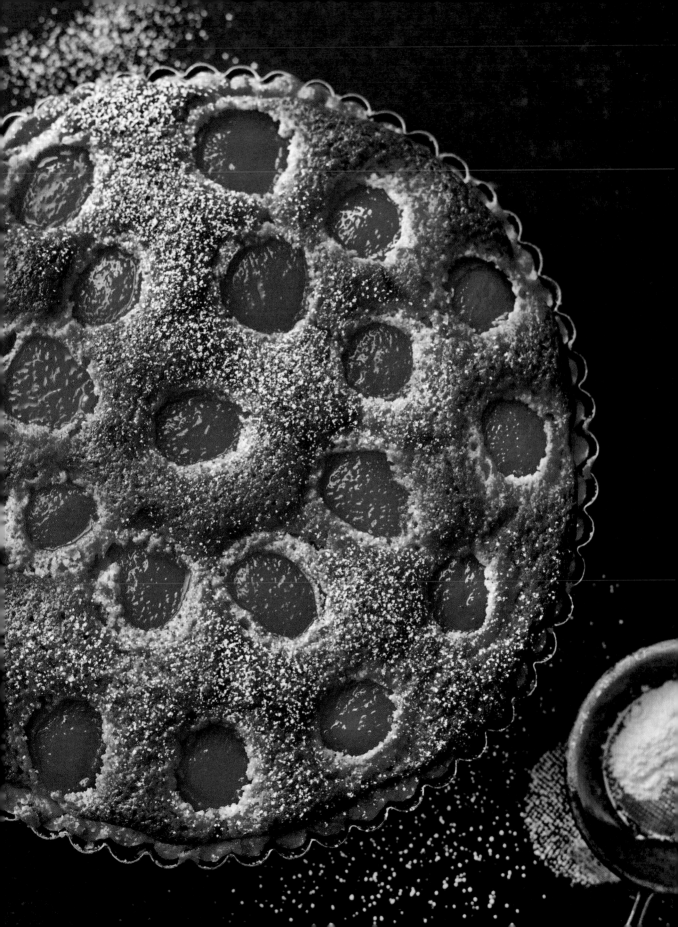

PEANUT BLONDIE PIE

*I made this with Richard in mind. He loves anything nutty, so with
the hint of hazelnut and the kick of peanuts, all brought together
with a drizzle of dark chocolate, this should hit the spot.*

½ **quantity of shortcrust
pastry (see page 132)
or 250g ready-rolled
shortcrust pastry**
plain flour for rolling out
1 heaped tbsp Nutella

Blondie filling
**120g white chocolate,
roughly chopped**
130g unsalted butter
150g caster sugar
100g plain flour
100g self-raising flour
2 large eggs, beaten
**1 tsp vanilla extract
or vanilla bean paste**
4 tbsp crunchy peanut butter
**50g good-quality dark
chocolate, chopped**

**You will also need a 25cm
tart tin with a depth of about
3.5cm and baking beans**

Preheat the oven to 190°C/375°F/Gas Mark 5.

Lightly dust the work surface with plain flour and roll
out the pastry into a circle with a thickness of about
2mm. Line the tart tin and push the pastry into the
corners. Trim off any excess pastry. Prick the base
of the tart shell with a fork. Screw up a sheet of baking
parchment and line the inside of the pastry case.
Chill for 10 minutes in the freezer.

Tip baking beans into the case and blind bake in
the middle of the oven for 15 minutes or until pale
golden in colour.

Take out of the oven, remove the baking parchment and
baking beans, and spread over the Nutella in an even
layer. Turn the oven down to 170°C/325°F/Gas Mark 3.

Melt the white chocolate and butter together in
a heatproof bowl over a pan of simmering water.
Stir until smooth and leave to cool slightly.

Tip the sugar and flours into a large bowl and make a well
in the middle. Add the eggs, vanilla and peanut butter to
the melted chocolate in the pan, stir to combine and pour
into the dry ingredients. Mix together until smooth.

Spoon the firm batter into the tart tin and spread level.
Place on a baking tray and cook on the middle shelf
of the oven for 30–35 minutes until golden.

Leave to cool completely in the tin.

Melt the dark chocolate in a sandwich bag (see page
249), snip the end and drizzle over the tart in a zigzag
fashion. Leave to set and then slice.

APPLE, GOOSEBERRY AND ELDERFLOWER CRUMBLE

My dad's the sort of dad every girl should have: he never judges, but is always there when you need him. He hasn't got a very sweet tooth, so while devising the recipes for this book I decided to make one that would be perfect for him. The natural sweetness of dessert apples is balanced perfectly by the fruity sharpness of cooking apples and gooseberries. It's delicious served with cold cream or hot custard. I use crushed sugar cubes for texture and sweetness.

600g cooking apples, peeled and cored
200g dessert apples, peeled and cored
50g caster sugar
50ml elderflower cordial
200g gooseberries
150g plain flour
100g ground almonds
130g unsalted butter, chilled and diced
100g white sugar cubes, roughly crushed in a sandwich bag with a rolling pin

You will also need an ovenproof pie dish

Preheat the oven to 200°C/400°F/Gas Mark 6.

Dice all of the apples and mix together with the caster sugar and cordial. Tip into the pie dish and tumble the gooseberries over the top.

To make the crumble, combine the flour, almonds, butter and crushed sugar cubes in the bowl of a food processor and pulse until you have a crumble texture. Sprinkle over the fruit and bake for 30–35 minutes until the fruit is bubbling and the crumble is golden.

Leave to stand for 5 minutes before serving.

PEACH AND BLUEBERRY CRUMBLIES

Baked peaches and blueberry compôte, topped off with a crispy, crunchy, crumbly topping. The compôte and crumble can be made in advance and then simply spooned over the gorgeous plump peaches. Tinned peaches are fine to use – the juice can be poured over the finished crumble.

6 peach halves
125g blueberries
100g caster sugar
finely grated zest and
    juice of 1 large orange
50g demerara sugar
generous pinch of sea salt
150g plain flour
75g unsalted butter,
    diced and chilled
60g finely chopped pecans
clotted cream, to serve

You will also need 6 ramekins
(glass ones look pretty)

Preheat the oven to 180°C/350°F/Gas Mark 4.

Place one peach half into each ramekin, cut side up.

Tip the blueberries and caster sugar into a saucepan over a medium heat. Cook over a gentle heat to allow the sugar to dissolve and the blueberries to soften and burst. Add the orange zest and half the juice and stir to combine and cook for another minute. Pour the compôte over the peach halves.

Tip the demerara sugar, salt and flour into a large bowl and, using the tips of your fingers, rub in the diced butter until the mixture resembles coarse breadcrumbs. You could also do this in the bowl of a food processor fitted with a metal blade and using the pulse function. Stir in the chopped pecans and sprinkle the mixture evenly over the fruit.

Bake in the preheated oven for 25–30 minutes until the crumble is golden. Leave to stand for 5 minutes and serve with clotted cream.

Crumbles, tarts and pithiviers

LEMON, ALMOND AND HONEY TARTS

*Crisp pastry, sticky gooey almonds and sweet and sharp lemon icing:
I love the contrasting textures and flavours in these tarts.*

½ **quantity of sweetcrust
pastry (see page 114)**
plain flour for dusting

Filling
55g unsalted butter
50g granulated sugar
2 tbsp runny honey
1 tbsp double cream
85g flaked almonds

Icing
150g icing sugar
**finely grated zest and
juice of 1 large lemon**

**You will also need a
12-hole patty tin and
a 7.5cm round cutter**

Preheat the oven to 180ºC/350ºC/Gas Mark 4.

Lightly dust the work surface with flour and
roll out the pastry until it is no more than 2mm
thick. Stamp out 12 circles and press one disc
into each patty tin.

Melt the butter, sugar and honey together
in a heavy-based saucepan until the sugar has
dissolved. Bring to the boil and remove from
the heat.

Stir in the cream and almonds and leave to cool
completely. Divide the mixture between the patty
tins and bake on the middle shelf of the oven for
20 minutes or until golden.

Leave to cool in the tins for 10 minutes before
transferring to a wire rack to cool completely.

Make the icing by mixing the icing sugar with
enough lemon juice to create a thick paste. Drizzle
or pipe over the cooled tarts and sprinkle with
the lemon zest to decorate.

GYPSY TART

A lady who attended my class while I was writing this book said it was really hard to find a good recipe for gypsy tart – I hope I've ended her search! I've added some lemon cream to cut through the sweetness.

For the lemon pastry
250g plain flour, plus
    extra for rolling out
125g unsalted butter,
    chilled and diced
25g icing or caster sugar
pinch of sea salt
2 large egg yolks
finely grated zest
    and juice of 1 lemon
2–3 tbsp double cream
    or milk (optional)

To make the pastry, put the flour, butter, sugar and salt into the bowl of a food processor fitted with a metal blade. Whizz with the pulse button until you have a breadcrumb consistency.

Add the egg yolks, whizz briefly, then add half the lemon juice, 1 tbsp at a time, until the dough comes together. If you need any extra liquid, add the cream or milk.

Turn on to a lightly floured work surface and work very briefly using your hands until the dough is smooth. Flatten into a disc, wrap in cling film and chill for at least 1 hour.

Preheat the oven to 200°C/400°F/Gas Mark 6.

The dough will be really soft, so roll between two sheets of baking parchment into a neat disc the thickness of £1 coin. Carefully line the tart tin, being sure to push the pastry neatly into the corners and trimming off the excess pastry from the top. Prick the base of the tart shell several times with a fork. Screw up a sheet of baking parchment and use to line the inside of the pastry case. Chill for 10 minutes in the freezer.

Filling
**410ml tin of evaporated
  milk, chilled**
340g dark muscovado sugar

Lemon cream
200ml double cream
75g mascarpone
finely grated zest of 1 lemon

**You will also need a 25cm tart
tin, baking beans and a piping
bag fitted with a star nozzle**

Tip the baking beans into the lined pastry case and blind bake on the middle shelf of the oven for 18–20 minutes until the pastry turns a pale golden colour. Remove the parchment and beans.

Meanwhile, in the bowl of a free-standing mixer or with an electric hand-held whisk, beat the evaporated milk and sugar together for at least 10 minutes until doubled in size, and light and fluffy. Pour the mixture into the blind-baked pastry case and return to the oven for 10 minutes – the surface of the tart will still be sticky but it will continue to set as it cools.

Leave to cool and then chill in the fridge for at least 1 hour or ideally overnight.

Whisk together the cream, mascarpone, lemon zest and remaining lemon juice until stiff peaks and spoon into the piping bag. Pipe star rounds on top of the chilled tart and cut into slices.

CHICKEN AND RED PEPPER PITHIVIER

A pithivier is a freeform pie, with a pastry top and bottom. I love the shape of this, such a gorgeous picnic table treat but equally as fab on a buffet table or for tea served with a simple salad. It would be an ideal way to use leftover roast turkey at Christmas, too.

2 tbsp olive oil
1 tsp butter
1 medium red onion,
    finely diced
4 medium red peppers,
    deseeded and roughly
    chopped
1 tsp dried thyme
150g cooked chicken, shredded
100g Cheddar, roughly chopped
plain flour for rolling out
1 quantity of rough puff pastry
    (see page 133) or 500g block
    ready-rolled puff pastry
1 egg yolk, beaten with
    1 tbsp milk

You will also need
a baking tray

Preheat the oven to 200°C/400°F/Gas Mark 6. Heat the olive oil and butter in a heavy-based frying pan and slowly sauté the diced onion for 10–12 minutes until softened.

Add the peppers and thyme and continue to sauté until softened. Remove from the heat and stir through the chicken and Cheddar, then leave to cool.

Divide the pastry into 2 halves. Lightly dust the work surface with flour and roll out each piece to a thickness of around 3mm. Cut the rolled pastry into one 23cm and one 25cm diameter disc.

Place the smaller disc on the baking sheet and pile the cooled filling into the centre, leaving a 1cm border around the edge.

Brush the edge with a little egg wash and place the remaining disc of pastry on top of the filling. Press the pastry edges together to seal, using a fork, pushing out any air bubbles as you go. Crimp the edges with finger and thumb to create the pithivier's trademark petals, and using a small sharp knife lightly score the top of the pastry in neat swirls from the centre. Brush with the egg wash.

Bake in the oven for 18–22 minutes until golden and well risen.

Leave to rest for at least 5 minutes before slicing.

Chapter six

QUICHES, PASTIES, PIES AND SAVOURY PUDDINGS

This is real comfort food at its best. Whenever I post a nursery-type recipe such as these on my blog, it gets record views. For the puddings and pies, always give yourself enough time to slow-cook the meats and use good ingredients. You can use shop-bought all-butter pastry for each of the recipes, but if you have time, homemade pastry is best.

SHORTCRUST PASTRY

The mainstay of most pastry recipes, it's always good to have a shortcrust pastry in your baking repertoire. I never use margarine in my pastry, as butter produces a far superior flavour and texture.

250g plain flour, plus
    extra for rolling out
125g unsalted butter,
    chilled and diced
pinch of sea salt
1 large egg yolk
2–3 tbsp water, chilled

Put the flour, butter and salt into the bowl of a food processor with a metal blade.

Whizz using the pulse button until you have a breadcrumb consistency.

Add the egg yolk, whizz briefly, then add the water a tablespoon at a time until the dough starts to come together to form a ball.

Turn out onto a floured surface and work the dough very briefly with your hands until it is smooth. Flatten into a disc, wrap in cling film and chill for at least half an hour before using.

ROUGH PUFF PASTRY

This produces a really light, flaky pastry. I know the method might seem a bit of a faff, but I'm sure you will agree once you've tasted the finished product that it is well worth the extra time and effort.

300g plain flour, plus extra for rolling out
pinch of sea salt
250g unsalted butter, very chilled or
125g unsalted butter and 125g lard, very chilled
ice-cold water

Tip the flour and salt into a large mixing bowl. Roughly grate the butter (or butter and lard) into the flour, holding the butter in its packet and pulling it down as you go. Using a palette or round-edged knife, flick the flour over the grated fat until all of the pieces are covered. Add enough ice-cold water to bring the dough together using the knife.

Turn the dough out onto a floured work surface and bring together briefly using your hands. Flatten into a rectangle, wrap in cling film and chill for 30 minutes.

On a lightly floured work surface, roll the dough out into a rectangle roughly 50 x 15cm. With one of the shorter sides of the rectangle nearest to you, fold the top third down into the middle and the bottom third up over this. You should now have a square measuring one-third of the original size but 3 times as thick. Make a small mark in the dough to indicate which side is top of the dough square. Wrap in cling film and chill for another 30 minutes.

Unwrap the pastry and place the square on the work surface, with the mark at the top. Turn the square 90 degrees clockwise and roll out into a neat rectangle roughly 50 x 15 cm. Fold the top third down in the middle and the bottom third up over it as before. Make another mark in the top of the square and chill for another 30 minutes.

Repeat this process twice more, always making sure that the dough is turned 90 degrees before you start rolling, and chilling the dough in between turns.

CHOUX PASTRY

This pastry is made in a very different way to shortcrust and rough puff, as you have to melt the butter with water in a saucepan before beating in the flour. But it produces a lighter-than-light end result and can be used in a whole array of sweet and savoury dishes.

pinch of sea salt
150g unsalted butter, diced
350ml water
200g plain flour, sieved
6 large eggs, beaten

Place the salt, butter and water in a saucepan over a medium heat and heat gently until the butter has melted.

Bring to the boil and quickly add the flour. Remove from the heat and beat the mixture with a wooden spoon until the dough becomes smooth.

Return the pan to the heat and continue to beat for 1-2 minutes until the dough becomes glossy and comes away from the sides of the pan.

Transfer to the bowl of a free-standing mixer or large mixing bowl and leave to cool for 5 minutes. Add the eggs, a little at a time, beating well after each addition. The dough will become shiny and the consistency of a thick paste that will reluctantly drop off the wooden spoon. You might not need all the egg – the dough should be stiff enough to pipe.

Spoon into piping bags and use immediately.

THYME, CHEESE AND TOMATO QUICHE

I love nothing more than a girly lunch in the garden, and this is something I regularly make for my friends. Serve with a rocket and Parmesan salad, elderflower cordial with sparkling water, sunshine and laughter.

1 quantity of shortcrust
   pastry (see page 132)
plain flour for rolling out
1 tbsp olive oil and a knob
   of unsalted butter
1 medium onion,
   finely chopped
4 stalks of thyme
400ml double cream
4 large eggs
salt and freshly ground
   black pepper
100g Cheddar, grated
65g sunblush tomatoes
   (drained weight),
   roughly chopped

You will also need a 23cm
loose-bottomed flan tin
and baking beans

Preheat the oven to 180°C/350°F/Gas Mark 4.

On a lightly floured surface, roll out the pastry to a thickness of 2mm. Line each tin with the pastry, using a rolling pin to roll over the tops of the cases to trim any excess. Chill the tart cases for 20 minutes. Line the flan tin with the parchment paper and baking beans and blind bake on the middle shelf of the oven for 20 minutes. Remove the beans and parchment and bake for a further 10 minutes. Remove from the oven.

Meanwhile, melt the olive oil and butter in a frying pan, add the onions and thyme leaves and cook gently until soft and translucent. Remove from the heat.

Whisk together the cream, eggs, salt and pepper to taste, and half the grated Cheddar.

Tip the cooled onions and chopped sunblush tomatoes into the pastry case in an even layer. Pour over the egg custard and top with the remaining grated cheese. Bake in the oven for 30-35 minutes until golden and slightly wobbly in the centre.

Leave to set in the tin before turning out and cutting.

SAMPHIRE, PEA AND MINT QUICHE

This recipe, which is great as a starter, came about because I inherited a veggie patch with our house, and in that patch are mint, peas and asparagus, along with some carrots and soft fruits. Samphire is one of my favourite vegetables and the saltiness works really well here – if you can't find it (try your local fishmongers), replace with asparagus tips.

1 quantity of shortcrust pastry (see page 132)
plain flour for rolling out

Filling
2 tbsp ricotta
handful of fresh mint
3 large eggs
200ml double cream
finely grated zest and 1tbsp juice of 1 lemon
40g fresh or frozen (defrosted) peas
30g samphire, snipped into 2.5cm (1 inch) pieces

You will also need twelve 8cm round loose-bottomed tart tins and baking beans

Preheat the oven to 200°C/400°F/Gas Mark 6.

On a lightly floured surface, roll out the pastry to the thickness of no more than 2mm. Line each tin with the pastry, using a rolling pin to roll over the tops of the cases to trim any excess. Chill the tart cases for 20 minutes. Line each tin with a square of parchment paper and baking beans and blind bake for 12 minutes on the middle shelf until golden.

Remove and turn the oven down to 180°C/350°F/ Gas Mark 4.

Meanwhile, make the filling. Blitz together the ricotta and mint with a hand-held blender or food processor, or simply beat until smooth using a wooden spoon.

In a separate bowl, whisk the eggs, cream and 1 tbsp of the lemon juice together, then add the mint and ricotta mixture. Mix in the peas and pour into the pastry cases. You don't need to add salt to the mix because samphire is naturally salty.

Divide the samphire between the 12 cases and sprinkle with the lemon zest. Bake on the middle shelf in the oven for 10–12 minutes until the pastry is golden and the egg custard is just set.

CORNISH PASTY

When I was little we went on holiday to Cornwall with its beautiful beaches and yummy pasties, but my lasting memory is waking from a dream of spiders only to find the hugest one running along my face! A genuine Cornish pasty is D-shaped and always contains beef, swede, potato and onion.

500g beef chuck steak, chopped
   into £1 coin sized pieces
salt and freshly ground
   black pepper
1 small swede
1 potato (Maris Piper)
1 small white onion
1 quantity of shortcrust
   pastry (see page 132)
1 egg, beaten with 1 tbsp milk

**You will also need a baking tray
lined with baking parchment**

Season the steak with salt. Peel and slice the vegetables finely – I use the slicing side of a box grater but you could also use a mandoline – and mix together with the beef. Season again with salt and black pepper.

Preheat the oven to 200°C/400°F/Gas Mark 6.

Divide the pastry into four pieces and roll each out into a 20cm circle (about the size of a side plate). Place a quarter of the filling into the middle of each disc leaving a 2cm gap from the edge. Brush the edges of the pastry with water and bring the edges to meet up and over the top of the meat. Use your fingers to crimp and seal the pasty closed; repeat with the remaining pastry discs. Brush with egg wash and transfer the finished pasties to the lined baking tray and chill for 10 minutes.

Place the pasties in the oven, on the middle shelf, and bake for 15 minutes, then turn the oven down to 180°C/350°F/Gas Mark 4 and bake for a further 30-40 minutes or until the pastry is golden.

MINCED BEEF SUET-CRUST ROLL

I know suet has gone a little out of favour in the last few years, but I really love it. This reminds me of childhood suppers sitting at the breakfast bar arguing with my brother about who'd wash and who'd wipe.

350g plain flour, plus
    extra for rolling out
175g suet
pinch of salt
1–2 tbsp water, chilled

Filling
2 tbsp olive oil
1 red onion, diced
3 carrots, finely diced
2 tsp dried oregano
500g minced beef
1 tbsp Worcestershire sauce
salt and pepper
1 tbsp flour
100ml water

You will also need a baking tray lined with baking parchment

Start by making the filling. Heat the olive oil in a heavy-based frying pan and fry the onions, carrots and oregano over a medium heat for about 10 minutes until softened.

Add the minced beef and continue to fry until browned. Add the Worcestershire sauce, and salt and pepper to taste, then stir in the flour and water. Simmer on a low heat for 1 hour. Remove from the heat to cool.

To make the pastry, tip the flour, suet and salt into the bowl of a food processor with a metal blade. Whizz using the pulse button until you have a breadcrumb consistency.

Add the water, one tablespoon at a time, mixing between each addition until the dough comes together to form a ball. Turn onto a floured surface and work the dough briefly with your hands until smooth. Flatten into a disc, wrap in cling film and chill for at least half an hour before using.

Preheat the oven to 200°C/400°F/Gas Mark 6.

Roll out the pastry on a lightly floured surface to make a 25cm x 40cm rectangle. Spread over the cooled pie filling. Roll the mix into a tight roll, tucking under each end to neaten and to prevent the filling from escaping. Transfer to a parchment-covered baking tray and bake in the oven for 15 minutes. Lower the oven temperature to 190°C/375°F/Gas Mark 5 and continue to cook for a further 20–30 minutes until the pastry is cooked through and the filling is piping hot.

Quiches, pasties, pies and savoury puddings

BEEF AND ALE PIE

The ale, along with some thyme and a real slow cook, gives this pie a real depth of flavour; it is so good with horseradish mash. Just make sure you use a decent ale, one that you would be prepared to drink.

6 tbsp olive oil

20g unsalted butter

2 white onions, sliced

4 large carrots, sliced

2 stalks of celery, sliced

4 stalks of fresh thyme

2 bay leaves

3 tbsp plain flour, plus
   extra for rolling out

pinch of sea salt

1 tsp freshly ground
   black pepper

1.5kg braising steak, diced

1 250ml bottle of real ale

2 beef stock cubes

1 tbsp Marmite

knob of unsalted butter

1 quantity of rough puff
   pastry (see page 133)

1 egg yolk, beaten with
   1 tbsp milk

**You will also need a large
(about 25cm) deep pie dish**

TOP TIP

Add ½ tbsp of horseradish to your mash at the end and beat it through for an extra kick.

Preheat the oven to 120°C/250°F/Gas Mark 1.

In a large ovenproof pan, heat the oil with the butter. Add the sliced onions, carrots, celery and herbs and sauté over a medium heat for about 10 minutes or until just softened. Remove the vegetables from the pan using a slotted spoon and set aside on a plate.

Combine the flour, salt and pepper in a large sandwich bag. Add the diced beef and shake to coat. Brown the beef in the hot pan in batches, adding more butter and oil if the pan becomes dry.

Return the softened vegetables to the pan and pour in the ale. Use a wooden spoon to scrape any caught bits from the bottom of the pan, then add the stock cubes and Marmite. Stir well and bring to the boil, then cover and place in the oven for 3–4 hours, checking regularly and adding more water if the liquid is getting too low.

Once the meat is tender, remove from the oven, check the seasoning and add a knob of butter to give the pie mix a glossy shine. Transfer to the pie dish and leave to cool slightly.

Turn the oven up to 190°C/375°F/Gas Mark 5. On a floured work surface, roll the pastry out to be slightly larger than the top of the pie dish. Brush the edges of the dish with egg wash, cut a 1cm wide, long strip of pastry and stick it all around the rim of the pie dish. Brush this edge with egg wash and drape the pastry across the dish and crimp the edges to seal. Trim the edges, make a couple of pricks in the centre to allow the steam to escape.

Bake the pie in the oven for half an hour or until the pastry is golden brown.

Quiches, pasties, pies and savoury puddings

CHICKEN AND MANGO EMPANADAS

I love Barcelona: it's the place that introduced me to tapas, potatoes bravas, garlic prawns and, best of all, empanadas. How could I not try to recreate them when I got home?

1 tbsp olive oil
1 chicken breast, chopped
    into bite-sized pieces
2-3 small spring onions, sliced
3 tbsp mango chutney
plain flour for rolling out
½ quantity of shortcrust
    pastry (see page 132)
1 egg yolk, beaten with
    1 tbsp milk

**You will also need a baking
tray and an 8cm round cutter**

Preheat the oven to 200°C/400°F/Gas Mark 6.

In a frying pan, heat the olive oil and gently fry the chicken and spring onions for about 5 minutes until they start to caramelise. Add the mango chutney, stir to coat the chicken, then remove from the heat and leave the mixture to cool.

On a lightly dusted work surface, roll out the pastry to 2mm thickness and cut into 10 discs using the cutter. Spoon 1 heaped tsp of the cooled chicken mixture into one half of each circle. Brush the edges of the pastry with some water, fold over and crimp the edges with your fingers to seal. Brush lightly with egg wash, transfer to the baking tray and chill for 10 minutes.

Bake in the preheated oven for 15–18 minutes until golden.

Bits & Bobs

Steak, red pepper and mozzarella empanada
For one of my family's favourite variations of an empanada recipe, see page 249.

Quiches, pasties, pies and savoury puddings

CHICKEN AND LEEK PIE

My lot love this pie. When they were young, I would cut out letters and pictures from the pastry offcuts to put on the top of the pie. Seeing their smiling faces when they sat down to eat it made that extra 5 minutes well worthwhile.

20g unsalted butter

3 tbsp olive oil

4 rashers of streaky bacon

2 leeks, trimmed and sliced
    into discs

3 stalks of lemon thyme or
    1 tbsp of chopped tarragon

1kg cubed chicken breast
    and/or thigh

200ml boiling chicken stock

2 tbsp double cream

plain flour for rolling out

1 x quantity of shortcrust
    pastry (see page 132)

1 egg yolk beaten with
    1 tbsp milk

You will also need
a 25cm pie dish

Preheat the oven to 200°C/400°F/Gas Mark 6.

Heat the butter and 2 tbsps oil in a large frying pan.

Snip the bacon, using a pair of scissors, into small lardons, add to the pan and fry until they start to brown and crisp. Add the leeks and the thyme (or tarragon) and sauté over a medium heat until they soften.

With a slotted spoon, transfer the leeks and bacon to a plate and set aside. Turn up the heat in the pan, add the remaining tbsp of oil and fry the chicken until sealed all over. Return the leeks and bacon to the pan and cook the mixture over a medium heat for 5 minutes. Pour in the chicken stock and continue cooking until reduced by a third. Stir in the cream and transfer the mixture to the pie dish.

On a lightly floured work surface, roll out the pastry so that it is 2-3cm larger than the pie dish. Brush the edges of the dish with egg wash, cut a 1cm wide, long strip of pastry and stick it all around the rim of the pie dish. Brush this edge with egg wash and drape the pastry across the dish and crimp the edges to seal. Score lines across the top of the pie to create a diamond shape, brush with the egg wash and bake in the oven for 20–25 minutes until golden and the filling is bubbling.

ROQUEFORT, LEEK AND POTATO PIE

A great meat-free pie that's delicious eaten hot or at room temperature. You can even serve it without the pastry topping, if you'd prefer. A pastry funnel will let out the steam from the potatoes and leeks.

100g unsalted butter

2 leeks, trimmed and finely sliced

1kg potatoes, peeled and sliced into ½cm thick slices

50g Gruyère, broken in to chunks

100g Roquefort, broken into chunks

150ml double cream

pinch of freshly ground black pepper

plain flour for rolling out

1 quantity of rough puff pastry (see page 133) or 375g ready-rolled puff pastry

1 egg yolk, beaten with 1 tbsp milk

pinch of sea salt

You will also need a 25cm shallow pie dish, a pastry funnel and a baking tray

TOP TIP

If you don't have a pastry funnel, a metal icing nozzle works just as well.

Heat half the butter in a frying pan and sauté the leeks over a low to medium heat for 10 minutes until soft.

Meanwhile, bring a large pan of salted water to the boil and parboil the potatoes for 10–12 minutes until just starting to soften.

In a jug, mix the cheeses together with the cream, pepper and remaining butter.

Preheat the oven to 200°C/400°F/Gas Mark 6.

Drain the potatoes, combine with the leeks and pour into the pie dish. Pour over the cream and cheese mixture and stir gently to combine. Place the pie funnel in the middle of the filling. Leave to cool slightly, while you prepare the pastry.

On a lightly dusted work surface, roll the pastry out to form a circle just bigger than the pie dish. Brush the edges of the dish with egg wash, cut a 1cm wide, long strip of pastry and stick it all around the rim of the pie dish. Brush this edge with egg wash and drape the pastry across the dish and crimp the edges to seal. Create a hole for the steam from the funnel.

Brush with the remaining egg wash and sprinkle with the salt. Place the dish on the baking tray in the oven for 10 minutes, before turning the heat down to 180°C/350°F/Gas Mark 4 and baking for a further 25–30 minutes until the pastry is risen, golden and crisp.

Leave the pie to rest for 10 minutes before serving.

Chapter seven

QUICK AND SIMPLE

Baking is mainly for me about relaxation. I get real pleasure from locking myself in the kitchen and forgetting the housework, the accounts or the grocery shopping, and making something lovely. But sometimes you need a quick fix or somebody turns up unexpectedly – in which case, these are your guys. This chapter features recipes using everyday ingredients. From the cupboard to the table, these dishes can be made in about half an hour.

BASIC SCONES

I have been making these scones for as long as I can remember, and they work. My sister-in-law bought me a little book called Tea at the Ritz *about 18 years ago, and since then, with a small adjustment, the recipe has become a part of me.*

225g self-raising flour,
  plus extra for dusting
1 tsp cream of tartar
½ tsp bicarbonate of soda
1 tbsp caster sugar
pinch of salt
50g unsalted butter,
  chilled and diced
80ml double cream
50–70ml full-fat milk
1 egg yolk, beaten
4 tbsp granulated sugar

**You will also need a baking tray
lined with baking parchment
and a 5cm round cutter**

Preheat the oven to 200°C/400°F/Gas Mark 6.

Sift the flour, cream of tartar, bicarbonate of soda, caster sugar and salt together into a large bowl.

Rub in the butter with your fingers until the mixture resembles fine breadcrumbs. Gradually add the cream and enough milk to bring the mixture together using a knife. Finish by bringing the mixture together with your hands.

Turn out onto a lightly floured work surface and give the mixture a little knead for 20 seconds (any more will make tough scones), then roll out the dough to a thickness of 2–3cm.

Using the cutter, cut into rounds and place on the prepared baking tray. Gather the dough scraps together, lightly press into a ball and re-roll to stamp out more scones. Brush with the beaten egg and sprinkle with the granulated sugar.

Bake on the middle shelf of the preheated oven for 12–14 minutes until well risen and golden. Cool on a wire rack until ready to eat. These are best eaten on the day of baking.

ROCKY ROAD

These are truly the most simple and versatile no-bakes I know.
Literally anything works: dried fruits, biscuits, jelly sweets, marshmallows.
Simply make your choice, chuck it all in and chill. These are our favourite
flavours – I'd love to hear what you decide to add to yours.

400g milk chocolate, chopped
handful of mini marshmallows
3 broken digestive biscuits
handful of Rice Krispies

Optional fillings
Maltesers
chocolate bars (Mars,
    Crunchie, Milky Way)
Turkish Delight
Rolos
popcorn
nuts (peanuts, pistachios,
    macadamia)
dried fruit (apricots,
    cranberries, mango,
    cherries)

You will also need a 23cm
square, deep baking tin,
lined with baking parchment

Melt the chocolate in a heatproof bowl over
a pan of simmering water or carefully in a
microwave in 10-second bursts on a low setting.
Stir until smooth and leave to cool slightly.
Add the marshmallows, biscuits and Rice
Krispies and stir to combine.

Choose a mixture of 3 or 4 different fillings
(at least one fruit and one chocolate), with a
variety of different textures, take a handful of
each and roughly chop into bite-sized pieces
(if they aren't already). Stir into the chocolate,
marshmallows and Rice Krispies and spoon
the mixture into the lined tin.

Chill until solid and cut into squares with
a knife warmed in hot water.

EASY ITALIAN SODA BREAD

I love the Med and here I have tried to combine all its flavours in a really simple, quick-to-make bread, perfect to serve at a summer barbecue. When I was testing this bread, my son Billy took it over to his friend Tom's house and apparently it was gone in 60 seconds.

1 tsp mixed dried herbs
220g plain flour
½ tsp bicarbonate of soda
180ml buttermilk
30ml olive oil
40g roasted red peppers
   (deseeded, from a jar),
   thinly sliced
50g mozzarella, torn

Toppings
a pinch or two of sea salt
8-10 basil leaves
2tbsps olive oil

**You will also need a 20cm
sandwich tin, greased and
lined with baking parchment**

Preheat the oven to 200°C/400°F/Gas Mark 6.

Tip the herbs, flour, bicarbonate of soda and buttermilk into a bowl and mix quickly using your hands.

Add the olive oil and bring together to form a dough. Press into the lined tin and stud with the roasted peppers. Place the torn mozzarella directly over the peppers, to protect them from the direct heat, and bake in the oven for 18–22 minutes or until the mozzarella is melted and golden.

Leave to cool in the tin for 5 minutes before transferring to a wire rack to cool. Best served still warm, drizzled with more olive oil and sprinkled with salt and basil leaves.

APPLE TURNOVERS

These remind me of Saturdays at my Nanny Jessie's with all the aunties and cousins in her tiny kitchen. The noise must have been horrendous but my nan had the biggest smile on her face, and that's something I'll always remember.

375g ready-rolled puff pastry
4 tbsp apple sauce from a jar
1 eating apple, peeled, cored and finely diced
1 egg yolk, beaten
caster sugar, to dust

You will also need a baking sheet and an 11cm round cutter

Bits & Bobs

Sweet pastry straws
Although I hate waste, you can't re-roll puff pastry as it will destroy the lovely layers that have been created. See page 249 for a chef's treat.

Preheat the oven to 190°C/375°F/Gas Mark 5.

On a lightly floured work surface, roll out the pastry and cut it into 6 discs using the cutter. Be careful not to twist the cutter as this will affect how the pastry rises.

Mix the apple sauce and chopped apple together and place a spoonful onto each pastry disc, covering one half and leaving a 1cm border. Brush the border with a little cold water and fold over the pastry, like mini pasties, and use your fingers to crimp them shut.

Brush the turnovers with the beaten egg yolk and sprinkle with caster sugar. Chill in the fridge for 10 minutes, then bake in the preheated oven for 10–12 minutes until golden.

SULTANA FAIRY CAKES

These little cakes remind me of my Auntie Helen. If you turned up at her home on the gorgeous Kent coast, she would knock some up and within minutes you'd be scoffing one (or three) along with a cup of tea and a chat. Everyone should have an auntie like her.

175g caster sugar
175g margarine, softened
3 large eggs, beaten
175g self-raising flour
75g sultanas
icing sugar for dusting

You will also need 2 bun trays lined with paper bun cases

Preheat the oven to 180ºC/350ºF/Gas Mark 4.

Cream the sugar and margarine together until pale, light and fluffy in the bowl of a free-standing mixer, with a hand-held electric whisk, or, if you're feeling energetic, with a wooden spoon.

Gradually add the eggs, mixing well between each addition and adding a teaspoon of the flour to the mixture if it starts to curdle.

Add the flour and stir to just combine, then fold in the sultanas until thoroughly combined.

Spoon the mixture into the paper cases, filling each one about half full. Bake on the middle shelf of the oven for 15–20 minutes until golden brown and well risen. A skewer should come out clean when inserted into the middle of the cakes.

Remove the cakes from the tins and leave to cool completely on a wire rack. Dust with icing sugar to serve.

FRUIT AND NUT BROWNIES

My brother Jay has a thing about brownies, so I thought I would devise this recipe for him. They're lovely and moist and squidgy and remind me of a fruit and nut bar.

50g blanched hazelnuts
100g good-quality dark
   chocolate, chopped
85g milk chocolate, chopped
115g unsalted butter, diced
300g caster sugar
1 tsp vanilla extract
   or vanilla bean paste
2 large eggs, beaten
100g plain flour
50g self-raising flour
30g cocoa powder
75g raisins

**You will also need a 20cm
square baking tin, greased and
lined with baking parchment**

Preheat the oven to 170°C/325°F/Gas Mark 3.

Tip the hazelnuts onto a small oven tray and toast in the oven for 5 minutes until pale golden. Remove from the heat, cool slightly and roughly chop.

Combine the dark and 25g of the milk chocolate in a large heatproof bowl. Add the butter and melt together carefully over a pan of simmering water or in a microwave in 20-second bursts on a low setting. Stir until smooth and combined and leave to cool slightly.

Add the sugar, vanilla and beaten eggs to the melted chocolate and butter and mix to combine.

Sift both flours and the cocoa powder into the bowl and mix until smooth. Fold in the toasted hazelnuts, raisins and remaining 60g of milk chocolate and spoon into the prepared tin. Spread level with a palette knife and bake on the middle shelf of the preheated oven for 30–35 minutes until the top is set but the inside of the brownie will still have some give.

Leave to cool in the tin and then cut into squares.

CHUTNEY AND CHEDDAR PALMIERS

When I was pregnant with Billy, I met a wonderful group of friends. We would meet every Tuesday post-birth, chat, eat cake and generally keep each other sane. My friend Pat (we call her Posh Pat because she lives in the most amazing house on the top of a hill, is very intelligent and speaks very well) always used to make palmiers, the delicious, heart-shaped pastries. So, here are my Posh Pat palmiers!

375g ready-rolled puff pastry
plain flour for rolling out
2 tbsp caramelised onion
    chutney
75g Cheddar, grated

You will also need a large baking tray lined with baking parchment

Preheat the oven to 190°C/375°F/Gas Mark 5.

Roll the pastry out on a floured surface into a 3mm deep rectangle so that one of the longest edges is closest to you and spread with the chutney in an even layer. Sprinkle over the Cheddar.

Starting at the furthest long edge, roll the pastry tightly down towards you until it reaches the middle. Then roll the bottom edge up to meet the top of the first roll. Press the rolls together to seal. and create the distinctive palmier shape.

Trim the ends and slice into 14 slices, each 1.5cm wide. Use a sharp, clean cutting motion, rather than a see-saw action, as this will affect how the palmiers rise. Place each slice cut side down on the lined baking sheet and flatten gently with the palm of your hand.

Chill for at least 10 minutes before baking in the preheated oven for 15 minutes until caramelised, golden and risen. Serve while still warm.

COFFEE AND WALNUT TRAYBAKE

This is my homage to Mary Berry, the traybake queen. She is to me, the most wonderful lady: an institution, somebody who my admiration for has no boundaries, beautiful inside and out.

175g caster sugar

175g margarine or unsalted butter, softened

175g self-raising flour

3 large eggs

1 shot of espresso (or 1 tsp instant coffee with 1 tbsp boiling water)

80g walnuts, finely chopped

Icing

2 shots of espresso (or 2 tsp instant coffee with 2 tbsp boiling water)

roughly 300g icing sugar

12 walnut halves

You will also need a 20 x 30cm baking tin, greased and lined with baking parchment

Preheat the oven to 170°C/325°F/Gas Mark 3.

Tip the sugar, butter or margarine, flour and eggs into the bowl of a free-standing mixer and beat for 2 minutes until smooth. If you don't have a free-standing mixer, you can use an electric hand-held mixer.

Add the espresso and walnuts and mix until combined. Pour the batter into the prepared tin, spread level using the back of a spoon or a palette knife and bake on the middle shelf of the preheated oven for 25–30 minutes until a skewer comes out clean when inserted into the middle of the cake. Leave to cool in the tin.

Meanwhile, mix together the coffee with enough icing sugar to make a thick paste. Pour over the cake and decorate with the walnut halves. Leave the icing to set, then cut into 12 slices or squares and serve.

AMERICAN PANCAKES

My lot love pancakes. They have always been our Saturday-morning favourite, and another treat that my nephew and the boys' friends always mention when they talk about sleepovers at ours. Frazer told his mum that Jo makes pancakes that are 'not from a bottle'. As long as you use the same teacup for each measurement, this will work perfectly.

3 large eggs
1 teacup full-fat milk
30g unsalted butter, melted
1 tbsp maple syrup
1 teacup self-raising flour
12 slices of streaky pancetta
    or smoked bacon
sunflower oil and unsalted
    butter, to cook
maple syrup, to serve

You will also need a baking tray

Preheat the oven to 200ºC/400ºF/Gas Mark 6.

Separate the eggs and whisk the whites to a soft peak.

Mix together the egg yolks, milk, melted butter and syrup in a jug. Put the flour into a large bowl and pour in the egg mix. Using a large metal spoon fold 1 tablespoon of the whipped egg whites into the mixture, then fold in the remainder carefully until combined.

Place the pancetta on the tray and bake in the preheated oven for 8–10 minutes until crisp.

Heat a splash of oil and a knob of butter in a large non-stick frying pan over a medium heat. Using a large spoon, drop three spoonfuls of batter into the pan to make 3 pancakes. Cook for about 40 seconds until the bubbles have stopped appearing on the top of the pancakes and the underside is golden. Flip the pancakes over and cook the other side until golden brown.

Remove from the pan and keep warm. Continue in the same way until all the batter has been used up, adding more oil to the pan if needed.

Warm the maple syrup in a pan or in the microwave. Drizzle over the pancakes and top with the hot and crispy pancetta.

Chapter
eight

SPECIAL OCCASIONS

*For me, special occasion baking is about creating
memories of those landmark days that you want to
stand out in your mind for ever: whether it's a special
Easter cake named after a beautiful niece; a duck
birthday cake that still brings a smile 17 years after
the first time you made it; or the Christmas cake
recipe that you've tweaked over the years so
that it's now perfect for you.*

BEEF WELLINGTON

This is my favourite dinner party dish. The recipe has evolved over the years, but the key is to make sure the meat is totally cold before wrapping it in the pastry or you will have a soggy bottom, for sure. I had my friends over for dinner recently and my friend Di told me I had to say that this is 'yum yum Piggy's bum!'

1 clove of garlic

1.2kg beef fillet (ask the butcher to remove any sinew)

1 tbsp fresh thyme leaves

sea salt and freshly ground black pepper

2 tbsp olive oil

60g unsalted butter

150g mixed mushrooms (I like oyster, shitake and portobello), chopped

1 tbsp Madeira wine, sherry or port

1 tbsp polenta

2 quantities of rough puff pastry (see page 133) or 750g ready-rolled puff pastry

85g farmhouse pâté

1 egg yolk, beaten with 1 tbsp milk

You will also need a large baking tray

Season the beef with salt and freshly ground black pepper and sprinkle with the thyme leaves.

Heat half the oil and the butter in a large frying pan over a high heat and brown the fillet for 3 minutes on each side and for 1 minute for each end – it should take about 14 minutes in total. Remove from the pan, loosely wrap in foil and leave to cool completely.

Chop the mushrooms. In the same pan that you used to brown the beef, heat the remaining oil and butter over a high heat, add the chopped garlic and mushrooms and fry until tender. Add the Madeira, season and reduce the heat to low. Continue to fry until the liquid has reduced and the mushrooms are cooked – this should take 8-10 minutes. Leave the mushrooms to cool.

Sprinkle a large sheet of baking parchment with the polenta and lay the first packet of ready-rolled pastry on top. Spread the pâté onto the middle of the pastry and place the cold beef on top. Reserve any juices from the rested beef for gravy.

I like to construct my beef Wellington on parchment paper so I can lift the whole thing easily onto the baking tray without making any mess!

Place the cooled mushrooms on top of the fillet and lightly brush the pastry around the the beef and pâté with water.

Take the second packet of ready-rolled pastry and drape it across the fillet and carefully wrap and tuck it in and around the beef so there are no trapped pockets of air. Using a kitchen knife or pizza wheel, trim off any excess pastry from around the bottom leaving an edge of about 1-2cm all around the beef. Seal the pastry by pressing the edges together with a fork. Use any trimmings to decorate the Wellington however you like. Brush the whole Wellington with egg wash, transfer to a baking tray and place in the fridge for 1 hour to chill.

About 20 minutes before you are ready to bake the Wellington, preheat the oven to 200°C/400°F/gas mark 6.

For medium beef, bake in the preheated oven for 35-45 minutes until the pastry is golden and a metal skewer comes out hot when inserted into the centre of the meat for 10 seconds. Let the Wellington rest for a further 10 minutes on the side before serving.

GOAT'S CHEESE AND FIG GOUGÈRES

Traditional gougères are gorgeous light puffs of choux pastry filled with a soft, creamy, cheesy filling with just a hint of bacon. The first time I tried them was in a little restaurant in Essex where Richard and I had the most lovely meal, with perfect food, great wine and fab company. As usual, here's my take on the dish.

½ quantity of choux pastry (see page 134)
4 dried figs, roughly chopped
200g soft crumbly goat's cheese
pinch of freshly ground black pepper
sunflower oil, for deep-frying
runny honey, to serve

TOP TIP
If making in advance, cook the gougères as above and store in the fridge until needed, then bake in the oven for 6–8 minutes at 200°C/400°F/Gas Mark 6. Just remember not to overcrowd the baking tray.

Place the choux pastry into a bowl, add the figs, goat's cheese and black pepper and beat until well combined.

Pour the sunflower oil (enough to cover the depth of a large grape) into a large frying pan – to test the temperature, add a small cube of bread to the hot oil and it should sizzle and turn golden in 15 seconds.

Using two teaspoons, carefully drop small balls of the cheesy dough into the oil and fry in batches for 3-4 minutes until they are golden all over. Keep turning the balls in the oil and don't overcrowd the pan.

Drain using a slotted spoon and leave to cool slightly on kitchen paper. Serve while hot, drizzled sparingly with honey.

TOFFEE APPLE CROQUEMBOUCHE

Just before I began to think about this book, somebody asked for a suggestion using toffee and apple and this gorgeous dessert was born. I love how baking and cooking fires up the creative side in me. I love the combination of soft pastry and cool, fruity custard with the crispy threads of caramel that binds the choux buns together. Beware, this is quite a tricky and time consuming recipe, and the filling is best made and chilled in advance.

1 quantity choux pastry
(should make about 120
choux buns, see page 134)
1 ice cube
300g caster sugar

Filling
20g unsalted butter
5 Granny Smith apples,
peeled, cored and
finely diced
1 tsp ground cinnamon
50g demerara sugar

Crème patissière
3 large egg yolks
60g caster sugar
30g cornflour
400ml full-fat milk
2 tbsp Calvados or apple
liqueur if unavailable
300ml double cream

You will also need a piping
bag fitted with a plain nozzle,
3 baking trays lined with
baking parchment, a small
ovenproof dish and a 25cm
circular cake base

Preheat the oven to 190°C/375°F/Gas Mark 5.

Spoon the choux pastry into a piping bag and pipe into mounds about the size of a cherry tomato on the lined trays, leaving plenty of space for them to rise and spread and allowing for about 40 buns per tray. Place the ice cube in a small ovenproof dish in the base of the preheated oven to create some steam and bake the buns on the middle shelf for 15 minutes.

Remove the choux buns from the oven and carefully, using the point of a sharp knife, make a small incision in the base of each bun. Return to the oven for 3 minutes, then leave to cool completely on a wire rack.

To make the filling, melt the butter in wide, shallow pan over a medium heat. Add the diced apples, cinnamon and sugar and allow to bubble and soften for 8–10 minutes. Using a hand-held stick blender, blitz the mixture until completely smooth. Return the apple purée to the pan, place over a medium heat and reduce by a third until thick, stirring frequently to prevent the purée scorching on the bottom of the pan. Leave to cool.

To make the crème patissière, whisk the egg yolks in a bowl with the sugar, cornflour and a third of the milk until smooth.

Heat the rest of the milk in a medium pan until almost boiling, then pour it over the egg mixture, stirring constantly. Add the Calvados, return to the pan and cook, whisking constantly, until the mixture boils and thickens. Simmer for a further minute to cook out the flour.

Stir the cooled apple sauce into the crème patissière and transfer to a jug to cool slightly and cover the surface with cling film to prevent a skin forming. Chill until ready to use.

Lightly whip the double cream and fold into the apple crème patissière using a large metal spoon. Spoon the mixture into the other piping bag and fill the choux buns by piping into the pre-made holes, or by splitting each bun horizontally and filling them using a teaspoon.

Make the caramel by putting the 300g caster sugar in a pan with a splash of water and slowly letting it melt over a medium heat until the sugar has dissolved. Do not stir. Bring the mixture to a boil until it turns a light caramel colour. Remove from the heat.

Take each filled bun and carefully dip the top into the hot caramel. Place on the cake board and begin to build up the buns in a pyramid pattern. If the caramel begins to harden, gently reheat until it liquefies, being careful not to let the caramel darken. Using two forks, drizzle any leftover caramel over the top of the finished pyramid.

TEMPURA MUSTARD SAUSAGES

My friend Gavin took me to a really amazing restaurant on Liverpool Street in London called the Duck & Waffle recently. The views were amazing but the thing I remember most are the deep-fried battered sausages with a fiery mustard kick. This is my take on those – serve with a pot of mayonnaise and a beer.

10 chipolata sausages, twisted in the centre to halve
1 tbsp English mustard
1-3 tsp English mustard powder to taste
160g self-raising flour
pinch of sea salt
250ml cold sparkling water
sunflower oil, for deep-frying

Brush the sausages with the English mustard using a pastry brush.

Put the mustard powder, flour, salt and sparkling water into a large bowl and whisk until the batter is smooth.

Heat the sunflower oil (enough to cover the sausages) in a large deep fryer or large saucepan over a medium heat – to test the temperature, add a small cube of bread to the hot oil and it should sizzle and turn golden in 15 seconds.

Coat the sausages in the batter and carefully lower into the hot oil, 4 or 5 at a time – don't overcrowd the pan. Using a spoon, carefully drizzle extra batter over the frying sausages, to create a lace effect – these will create lovely crispy bits. Each sausage should take 4–5 minutes.

Remove and drain using a slotted spoon and leave to cool slightly on kitchen paper. Cook the remaining sausages in the same way. Eat while hot.

HALLOWEEN BISCUITS

*We always had such fun on Halloween when my boys were younger.
Where we live is very rural, so trick or treating was out of the question.
We always had a tea party instead when the boys were young – pin the
rib on the skeleton, musical bumps and, of course, a ghoulish tea.*

250g plain flour, plus
   extra for dusting
1 tsp baking powder
80g caster sugar
110g unsalted butter,
   diced and chilled
1 large egg, beaten
1 tsp vanilla extract
   or vanilla bean paste
250g ready to roll
   fondant icing
gel food colours
4 tbsp apricot jam,
   heated and sieved
tubes of royal icing
   sugar in assorted
   corresponding colours

**You will also need Halloween
cookie cutters in a variety of
shapes and baking trays lined
with baking parchment**

In a food processor, mix the flour, baking powder
and sugar until combined. Add the butter and
pulse again until incorporated. Add the egg and
vanilla and pulse again until the dough is smooth.

Turn the mixture out on to a lightly floured work
surface and bring together into a ball using your
hands. Flatten into a disc, cover with cling film
and chill for 30 mins.

Place the chilled dough between two pieces of
floured baking parchment and roll to the thickness
of a £1 coin. Using cutters, stamp out the shapes
and arrange on the prepared baking trays. Chill
on the baking trays in the freezer for 20 minutes.

Meanwhile, preheat the oven to 170°C/350°F/
Gas Mark 4.

Bake the biscuits on the middle shelf of the
preheated oven for 10–12 minutes until pale
golden. Remove, leave to firm and cool slightly
on the baking trays, then transfer to cool
completely on wire racks.

Meanwhile, divide the fondant icing into four
and tint with the gels. Knead until the colour is
consistent. Roll the icing on a craft mat or between
sheets of baking parchment to the thickness of
a £1 coin and cut out shapes corresponding to the
biscuits. Brush the biscuits with the heated, sieved
apricot jam and place the fondant shapes on top;
gently smooth out. Add any details with the tubes
of royal icing. Allow to dry for several hours.

MINCEMEAT STEAMED PUDDING

This is a really lovely, light alternative to a traditional Christmas pudding. It's also a great substitute if you haven't had time to make a traditional pud – with all the flavours of Christmas, I'm sure your guests won't complain.

200g luxury or
    homemade mincemeat
2 tbsp Cointreau or fresh
    orange juice
150g unsalted butter, softened
150g caster sugar
3 large eggs
150g self-raising flour
1 tsp ground cinnamon
3 tbsp full-fat milk

To serve
150g brandy butter (optional)

**You will also need a 1.2 litre
(2 pint) pudding basin, buttered**

**Bits
& Bobs**

Brandy butter
See page 249 for my recipe.
A welcome addition every
year at Christmas.

Mix the mincemeat with the Cointreau or orange juice until it slackens to a dropping consistency (you might not need all the liquid for it to drop off easily from a spoon). Spoon the mixture into the bottom of the buttered basin.

Tip the butter, sugar, eggs, flour, cinnamon and milk into a food processor and whizz until just combined and smooth.

Spoon the sponge mixture into the basin, making sure the mincemeat is completely covered. Spread level with the back of a metal spoon or a palette knife. Lay a sheet of baking parchment over the bowl, top with a sheet of foil and pleat the two together in the middle to allow space for the sponge to rise. Fold the paper and foil over the sides of the bowl and tie securely with kitchen string. Trim off any excess paper and foil but leave about 1-2cm below the string.

Put the bowl into a steamer, or a large saucepan with a saucer inverted on the bottom, pour boiling water to come halfway up the sides of the bowl and steam for 2 hours until the pudding has risen and a skewer inserted into the middle of the pudding comes out clean. Top up with boiling water to stop the pan drying out.

Run a palette knife around the edge of the sponge to loosen the sides and turn the pudding out of the bowl onto a warmed serving dish. Serve in wedges with the brandy butter spooned over the top.

PANFORTE

This traditional Italian treat of fruit and nuts will last for two weeks in an airtight container, so I like to make mine the weekend before Christmas so the boys can help themselves over the holidays. I recommend adding a touch of edible gold leaf – if you can't sparkle at Christmas, when can you!

90g demerara sugar
125g clear, runny honey
50g pistachios
50g blanched almonds
50g dried cherries, chopped
50g dried cranberries
50g dried apricots, chopped
50g raisins
50g dried figs, chopped
70g plain flour
40g cocoa powder
1 tsp ground cinnamon
edible gold leaf (optional)

You will also need a loose-bottomed 20cm cake tin, lined with baking parchment

Preheat the oven to 180ºC/350ºF/Gas Mark 4.

Heat the sugar and honey together in a small saucepan over a low heat, stirring until the sugar dissolves. Bring to the boil and simmer for 2 minutes. Remove from the heat and leave to cool slightly.

In a large bowl, mix together the nuts and dried fruit. Add the flour, cocoa powder and cinnamon, and stir to combine.

Add the cooled syrup and stir to combine.

The mixture will feel very stiff, so use your hands to knead the mixture into the tin. Flatten the top with your hands, to create an even layer, and bake in the centre of the preheated oven for 35-40 minutes until just firm to the touch.

Remove from the oven and ease the panforte out of the tin while still hot. Transfer to a wire rack to cool completely. Decorate with the gold leaf, if using, and slice into wedges to serve.

VALENTINE'S SALTED CARAMEL CHOCOLATE POTS

Some candles, a bottle of fizz, a nice dinner, followed by these creamy, silky chocolate pots ... mmm. I love that you can make these treats in the afternoon, then pop them in the fridge until you're ready to serve. If you don't like salted caramel, they will work just as well without the salt.

Salted caramel
100g soft light brown sugar
75ml double cream
15g unsalted butter
½ tsp sea salt

Chocolate
150ml double cream
75g good-quality dark chocolate, finely chopped
75g milk chocolate, finely chopped
1 large egg yolk

You will also need 2 deep glass ramekins or glasses

Start by making the salted caramel, by gently heating the sugar, cream, butter and salt in a pan until the sugar and butter has dissolved. Bring to the boil, reduce the heat to a simmer and reduce for 2 minutes until thickened, then pour into a shallow dish and chill for 2 hours.

Meanwhile, tip the chopped chocolates into a bowl, heat the cream until just boiling and pour over the dark and milk chocolate. Stir until the chocolate has completed melted.

Add the egg yolk and beat until the mixture is smooth and glossy. Pour half the mixture into the ramekins. Add a generous teaspoon of the salted caramel to each of the ramekins and top with the remaining chocolate mixture. Cover with clingfilm and chill in the fridge to set for 2-3 hours. Spare caramel can be kept in the fridge for 3-4 days and can be served warm with ice cream.

Remember – this recipe contains raw egg. Be careful who you feed it to!

Bits
& Bobs

White chocolate hearts
Pretty white chocolate hearts really finish a pudding. See page 249 for how to make them.

LITTLE DUCK BIRTHDAY CAKE

This was the cake I made for Dylan's first birthday. It's stood the test of time, as nearly 20 years later it delights my little nieces and nephews.

Cake
325g self-raising flour
325g unsalted butter, softened
275g caster sugar
6 large eggs
2 tsp vanilla extract or vanilla bean paste

Decoration
300g unsalted butter, softened
600g icing sugar
yellow gel food colouring
200g desiccated coconut
100g orange fondant icing
2 sweets for the eyes (I like using Liquorice Allsorts jelly buttons or Smarties)

You will also need a greased 1.7 litre (3 pint) ovenproof pudding basin and a greased 300ml (½ pint) ovenproof pudding basin

Preheat the oven to 170°C/325°F/Gas Mark 3.

Tip all of the cake ingredients into the bowl of a free-standing mixer and beat for 2 minutes until smooth. If you don't have a free-standing mixer, you can use an electric hand-held mixer.

Spoon the cake batter into the prepared basins filling each bowl two thirds full and spread level using a palette knife.

Bake on the middle shelf of the oven. The 300ml pudding basin will take 25–28 minutes, while the 1.7 litre basin will take 55–65 minutes. They should be well risen, golden and a skewer should come out clean when inserted into the middle of the cakes.

Leave each cake to cool in its pudding basin for at least 5 minutes before turning out onto a wire rack to cool completely.

To make the buttercream, beat the butter in the free-standing or electric hand-held mixer until light, creamy and smooth. Gradually add the icing sugar and a touch of yellow gel food colouring and beat on slow speed to combine.

Combine the coconut with a little yellow gel food colouring and using your hands mix through until combined and evenly coloured.

Cover each cake with the buttercream, spreading smoothly with a palette knife. Sprinkle the yellow coconut over to completely coat each cake so it looks like feathers. Arrange the cakes on a large serving dish or board with the smaller cake just in front of the larger one.

Divide the orange fondant into thirds – shape one into a bill, and the remaining two into the feet, and position on the body. Finish with the sweets for the eyes.

MINCE BAKEWELL TART

If we get invited out over the festive season, I will take one of these. It's always well received and looks really pretty, especially with a dusting of icing sugar.

75g unsalted butter, softened
100g caster sugar
1 large egg
1 tsp vanilla extract
   or vanilla bean paste
175g plain flour
pinch of sea salt

Filling
125g unsalted butter, softened
125g caster sugar
2 large eggs
40g ground almonds
110g self-raising flour
1 tsp mixed spice
1 400g jar luxury mincemeat
40g flaked almonds

You will also need a 23cm tart tin with a depth of about 3-5cm, baking beans and a baking tray

Cream together the butter and sugar until pale, light and fluffy using a free-standing mixer, using an electric hand-held mixer, or by hand with a wooden spoon. Mix in the egg and vanilla. Add the flour and salt and mix until combined into a clay-like dough. Flatten into a disc, wrap in cling film and chill for 1 hour.

Preheat the oven to 200°C/400°F/Gas Mark 6.

Roll out the dough between two sheets of baking parchment until 3mm thick and line the tart tin, making sure to push the dough into the corners. Prick the base of the tart shell with a fork. Screw up a sheet of baking parchment and use to line the inside of the pastry case. Chill for 10 minutes in the freezer.

Tip the baking beans into the lined pastry case and blind bake on the middle shelf of the preheated oven for 15 minutes until pale golden. Turn the oven down to 170°C/325°F/Gas Mark 3.

To make the filling, cream the butter, sugar, eggs, ground almonds, flour and spice in the bowl of a free-standing mixer or with a hand-held electric whisk. Beat until smooth, light and fluffy.

Spread the mincemeat onto the base of the tart in an even layer and spoon over the batter. Spread level, sprinkle over the flaked almonds, place on a baking tray and bake in the oven for 45–50 minutes until golden and firm.

Leave the tart to cool in the tin for 15–20 minutes and then transfer to a wire rack until cold.

EASTER MEADOW CAKE

My little nieces are called Layla and Meadow: they are true beauties with laughter like a warm summer's day. I've made this cake with them in mind. If you're feeling super-creative you could even make another farmyard animal out of fondant icing to keep the pigs company!

300g self-raising flour
1 ½ tsp baking powder
300g caster sugar
300g margarine
6 large eggs, beaten
2 large egg yolks
1 tsp vanilla extract
 or vanilla bean paste
2 heaped tbsp chocolate
 spread (Sainsbury's do
 a great chocolate popping
 candy spread)

Decoration
250g unsalted butter, softened
500g icing sugar
green gel food colouring
5 Flake chocolate bars
5 fluffy Easter chicks
9 Cadbury's Mini Eggs
sugarpaste flowers and
 butterflies

You will also need three 20cm sandwich tins, greased and lined with a disc of buttered baking parchment, and a piping bag fitted with a grass nozzle

Preheat the oven to 180°C/350°F/Gas Mark 4.

Tip all the cake ingredients into the bowl of a free-standing mixer and beat for 2 minutes until smooth. If you don't have a machine, you can use an electric hand-held mixer.

Divide the batter evenly between the prepared cake tins and spread level using a palette knife. Bake on the middle shelf of the preheated oven for about 25–30 minutes or until golden, well risen and a skewer inserted into the middle of the cakes comes out clean.

Remove from the oven and carefully turn the cakes out of the tins, peel off the parchment and leave to cool on wire cooling racks. Once completely cold, sandwich the cakes together with the chocolate spread. Place on a turning table or cake board.

Next, make the buttercream by creaming the butter in the mixer until smooth. Gradually add the icing sugar with the mixer on a slow speed until the buttercream is soft and light. Add green gel food colouring gradually until the buttercream is a vibrant grassy green. Transfer a third of the buttercream to a separate bowl and cover the cake with a crumb coat (see Top Tip).

Continued overleaf

A 'crumb coat' stops any of the cake crumbs getting into the finished icing and spoiling the look of the cake. Spread the separated buttercream third in a thin layer all over the cake and pop in the freezer for half an hour until set and no longer tacky.

Take half the remaining buttercream and using a palette knife spread roughly over the set crumb coat. Spoon the other half into the piping bag fitted with the grass nozzle and pipe around the base of the cake to cover the seam and create the meadow.

Slice the Flakes in half, and then again lengthways, and position on the sides of the cake to create a fence pattern.

Pipe the remaining icing on top to create a meadow effect, decorate with the chicks, Cadbury's mini eggs, butterflies and flowers – get creative!

ROSE AND CHOCOLATE WEDDING CAKE

*This is a really great way to make a spectacular-looking cake.
Fill with roses and you have the most perfect wedding centrepiece.*

Base
235g unsalted butter, softened
410g caster sugar
4 large eggs, beaten
105g self-raising flour
280g plain flour
13/4 tsp bicarbonate of soda
95g cocoa powder
280ml sour cream,
   at room temperature
   (see Top Tip page 220)
70g full-fat cream cheese,
   at room temperature

Top layer
100g unsalted butter, softened
165g caster sugar
2 large eggs, beaten
50g self-raising flour
115g plain flour
½ tsp bicarbonate of soda
45g cocoa powder
110ml sour cream,
   at room temperature
30g full-fat cream cheese,
   at room temperature

Preheat the oven to 180°C/350°F/Gas Mark 4.

Start by making the base cake. Beat the butter and caster sugar together until pale, light and fluffy using either a free-standing mixer or an electric hand-held mixer.

Gradually add the beaten eggs, a little at a time, beating well between each addition.

Sift both the flours, the bicarbonate of soda and the cocoa powder into a separate bowl. In a third bowl, mix the sour cream and cream cheese together until smooth. Add half the sifted dry ingredients to the egg and sugar mixture and fold in using a large metal spoon. Then add half of the cream mixture and combine. Repeat this process with the remaining flour and sour cream and mix until smooth.

Spoon the cake batter into the 25cm tin and spread level with a palette knife. Place on the middle shelf of the oven and bake for 70–80 minutes or until a skewer inserted into the middle of the cake comes out clean. Leave the cake to cool in its tin for 10 minutes before turning out onto a wire rack to cool completely. If making the day before, wrap the cooled cake in baking parchment and foil until ready to decorate.

Continued overleaf

Vanilla buttercream
750g icing sugar
350g unsalted butter, softened
1 tsp vanilla extract
   or vanilla bean paste

160 10cm tall dark
   chocolate cigarillos

40-70 small trimmed roses,
   unprayed and untreated

You will also need both a 15cm
and a 25cm round springform
or loose-bottomed cake tin,
each buttered and the bases
lined with a disc of buttered
baking parchment, a disposable
piping bag and 3 cake dowels

TOP TIP
As an alternative to the
roses, decorate with fresh,
soft fruits, such as raspberries,
strawberries, blueberries and
redcurrants. Add the fruits
at the very last minute.

Make the top layer by repeating the method
as above with the quantities listed. Spoon the
cake batter into the 15cm tin and spread level
with a palette knife. Place on the middle shelf
of the preheated oven for 40–45 minutes or until
a wooden skewer inserted into the middle of the
cake comes out clean. Leave the cake to cool in
its tin for 10 minutes before turning out onto
a wire rack to cool completely.

To make the buttercream, beat the butter, icing
sugar and vanilla extract until light and fluffy.
Cover the cooled cakes with the buttercream.
Place smaller cake onto a cake board then place
on the centre of the larger cake.

Working quickly, press the cigarillos around
the outside of the cakes, cutting in half for the
top layer. Add roses to finish.

CHRISTMAS CAKE

This is a light, spiced sponge, with all the flavours of Christmas baked in a gorgeous Christmas-y Bundt tin and dusted with a shower of icing sugar snow.

250g unsalted butter, softened
300g caster sugar
4 large eggs, beaten
3 tbsp maple syrup
150g mincemeat
100ml double cream
440g self-raising flour
1 tsp baking powder
1 tsp ground cinnamon
¼ tsp grated nutmeg
icing sugar to dust

You will also need a 23cm Christmas Bundt tin, well greased with cake-release spray or flavourless vegetable oil

Preheat the oven to 170ºC/325ºF/Gas Mark 3.

Cream the butter and sugar together in the bowl of a free-standing mixer or in a large bowl with a hand-held electric whisk until light and fluffy.

Gradually add the beaten eggs to the creamed butter, mixing well between each addition.

Add the maple syrup, mincemeat and cream and mix to combine.

Carefully fold in the flour, baking powder and spices using a large metal spoon. Pour into the prepared tin, spread level and bake in the preheated oven on the middle shelf for 55–70 minutes or until golden and a skewer inserted into the cake comes out clean. If you notice the cake is browning too quickly, loosely cover with foil.

Remove from the oven and leave to cool in the tin for 5 minutes and then carefully turn out onto a wire rack to cool completely.

Dust with icing sugar to serve.

PAVLOVA TOWER

Sometimes I'll make this meringue in beautiful pastel colours, but always I'll pile it high with lemon curd cream and soft fruits. You'll need to at least make the base meringue the day before you want to serve this, and construct the tower at the last minute for the best results. For a special touch, tumble rose petals all over the cake. You could use deep red roses for a ruby anniversary or for a silver or golden anniversary, use coloured, sugared almonds.

Base meringue
7 large egg whites,
    at room temperature
350g caster sugar
1 tsp cream tartar

Top tiers
7 large egg whites,
    at room temperature
350g caster sugar
1 tsp cream tartar

Raspberry cream
600ml double cream
6 tbsp raspberry conserve
250g raspberries

Lemon cream
300ml double cream
500g mascarpone
3 tbsp lemon curd
2 lemons

750g raspberries
500g strawberries, hulled
150g redcurrants
2 tbsp caster sugar
100g white chocolate, melted
yellow rose petals and sugared
    almonds (optional)

Preheat the oven to 150°C/300°C/gas mark 2.

Start by making the base meringue. Tip the egg whites into the spotlessly clean, dry bowl of a free-standing mixer fitted with a whisk attachment. Whisk the egg whites until they will hold a stiff peak. Gradually add the sugar, whisking constantly until it has all been incorporated and the meringue is thick and glossy. Add the cream of tartar and give a final quick whisk to thoroughly combine.

Spoon the meringue out onto the middle of the lined baking tray and spread into a round, approximately 30cm in diameter and using a palette knife to create elegant swirls on the side of the pavlova. Slide the baking tray onto the middle shelf of the preheated oven, immediately turn the temperature down to 100°C/ 200°F/gas mark ½ and bake for 3 and ½ hours until the meringue is pale and crisp. Turn off the oven and leave the meringue inside to cool completely.

To create the top tiers preheat the oven to 150°C/300°C/gas mark 2.

Prepare the meringue following the method above. Place one large scoop of the meringue into a piping bag fitted with an open-star nozzle and pipe a large kiss/swirl, about 5cm in diameter on one side of one of the prepared baking trays. This swirl/kiss will be the final layer of the finished pavlova tower.

You will also need 3 lipless baking trays lined with baking parchment and a piping bag fitted with an open-star nozzle

The perfect meringue
See page 249 for my trick for a meringue that always works.

Spread 1/3 of the remaining meringue into a round roughly 18cm in diameter onto the same baking sheet as the kiss. Spoon the remaining meringue onto another lined baking tray into another round roughly 25cm in diameter.

Slide the meringues on the middle and bottom shelves of the preheated oven, immediately turn the temperature down to 100°C/ 200°F/gas mark ½ and bake for 3 hours until the meringue is pale and crisp. Turn the oven off and leave the meringues to cool completely inside the oven.

Meanwhile, make the raspberry cream by whipping the double cream until it will hold a soft peak. Stir through the raspberry conserve and tumble in the raspberries. Cover with cling film and chill in the fridge until needed.

To make the lemon cream, whip the double cream to soft peaks. Fold through the mascarpone and lemon curd. Zest the lemons into long strands and fold through the cream. Cover with cling film and chill in the fridge until needed.

When ready to serve, tip the soft fruits into a large bowl, sprinkle with the sugar and toss gently to combine.

Take the largest meringue and brush the top with roughly 3 tablespoons of the melted white chocolate to create a seal. Repeat with the other two meringue layers and leave to set and the chocolate to harden.

Place the largest meringue onto the serving plate and top with ¾ of the raspberry cream and ⅓ of the macerated soft fruits. Top with the second meringue layer, spoon over the lemon cream and another ⅓ of the soft fruits.

Add the third meringue layer, spread with the remaining raspberry cream and soft fruits. Finally place the meringue kiss on top and decorate with rose petals or/and sugared almonds.

SUPPER BAKES

One-tray suppers are perfect for those evenings when you don't want a mountain of washing up; well, let's be fair, that's every evening! Don't be afraid to make these recipes your own, especially in this chapter, when weighing is a little less important. If there is a herb that you're not fond of, try one that you love.

RAGU PENNE BAKE

Slow-baked beef, tinned tomatoes and a few herbs, all mixed into some penne. Grate over some cheese and you have a meaty hug on a plate. Don't be scared to add the milk, it makes a lovely mellow ragu.

2-3 tbsp olive oil

800g braising steak, chopped into large diced chunks

1 carrot

1 onion

4 large cloves (or 6 small) of garlic

1 stick of celery

2 x 400g tins of chopped tomatoes

175ml glass white wine or chicken stock if preferred

2 beef stock cubes

2 tbsp Worcestershire sauce

1-2 stalks parsley

2 bay leaves

100ml full-fat milk

450g dried penne pasta (or 75g per person)

200g mozzarella, grated

100g Cheddar, grated

You will also need a large, roughly 28cm, ovenproof saucepan with a lid

Preheat the oven to 200°C/400°F/Gas Mark 6.

Heat half of the olive oil in the saucepan and add half of the beef. Brown the meat over a high heat. Remove from the pan and repeat with the remaining beef. Once all the meat is browned, remove from the pan and set to one side.

Place the carrot, onion, garlic and celery in the bowl of a food processor and blitz until finely diced. Add to the pan and gently fry for 5 minutes, adding more olive oil if needed.

Return the meat to the pan, add the tomatoes, wine, stock cubes, Worcestershire sauce and herbs. Season with salt and pepper, cover and cook in the preheated oven for 20 minutes.

Lower the temperature of the oven to 100°C/200°F/Gas Mark ½ and cook for a further 3-4 hours until the meat is tender and falling apart. After two hours of cooking remove the lid.

Return the pan to the stove, remove the parsley and bay leaves, and shred the meat roughly with a fork. Add the milk and leave to simmer.

Meanwhile, bring a large pan of salted water to the boil. Add the penne pasta and cook according to packet instructions until al dente. Drain and tumble into the ragu pan. Stir to combine and top with the mozzarella and Cheddar. Return to the oven for 15 minutes until the cheese topping is golden and gooey.

BEEF COBBLER

*My middle son, Jesse, has always loved a hearty stew or casserole
and he particularly likes dumplings so I thought I'd try this out on him.
The result was another family favourite.*

40g dried porcini mushrooms
3 tbsp olive oil
20g unsalted butter
2 tbsp plain flour
pinch of sea salt
1kg braising steak, roughly
    chopped into cubes
2 red onions, sliced
65g pancetta, cubed
2 tbsp fresh thyme, picked
1 tbsp garlic mayonnaise
¼ bulb of garlic, peeled
1 tbsp Worcestershire sauce
2 beef stock cubes

Cobbler
275g self-raising flour
handful fresh herbs
    (I like parsley)
110g unsalted butter,
    cold and diced
50g grated Cheddar
1-2 tbsp full-fat milk

You will also need a heavy-
bottomed casserole with
a lid and 5cm round cutters

Soak the porcini mushrooms in enough boiling
water to cover.

Heat 1 tablespoon of the oil in a large frying pan.
Mix the flour and salt together and use to lightly
coat the chopped steak. Cook the beef in batches
over a high heat for about 5 minutes until the meat
is sealed and brown. Remove from the pan and
tip into the casserole dish.

Add another tablespoon of the oil, a knob of the
butter, the red onions and pancetta to the pan
and cook over a medium heat until the onions
are softened and starting to caramelise. Transfer
to the casserole dish with the beef.

Strain the soaked mushrooms into a bowl, through
a new J Cloth or a very clean tea towel to remove
any grit. Reserve the stock. Add a little more oil
and butter to the frying pan and fry the drained
mushrooms and thyme leaves for 6–8 minutes
until tender. Season wth black pepper. Stir in the
garlic mayonnaise and remove from the heat.

Continued overleaf

Add the whole garlic cloves to the casserole dish, along with the fried mushrooms, and stir to combine. Add the strained mushroom water, Worcestershire sauce, stock cubes and enough boiling water to cover the meat. Simmer over a low heat, covered, for 1½–2 hours. Keep an eye on the liquid and top up with more boiling water if necessary.

After an hour and a half, preheat the oven to 190°C/375°F/Gas Mark 5 and make the cobbler mix. Tip the flour and herbs into a large bowl and season with salt and pepper. Add the butter and chop into the flour using a table knife. Stir in half the grated cheese and make a well in the middle of the ingredients. Add the milk 1 tablespoon at a time and gently incorporate to make a soft dough using a round bladed knife. You might not need all of the milk. Lightly dust the work surface with flour. Gently roll out the dough, being careful to not overwork the dough or the cobbler will be tough, and cut into 5cm rounds using the cutter.

Pop the cobbler pieces on top of the casserole, sprinkle over the remaining grated cheese and bake in the oven, without the lid, for 25–30 minutes until the cobbler is golden brown.

CHICKEN, PANCETTA AND MAPLE PARSNIP TRAYBAKE

Maple parsnips are one of my top 10 veggies, and they complement chicken, pancetta and a little thyme perfectly. I like to serve this with some green beans, which I chuck in the microwave and then serve drizzled with balsamic.

6 parsnips peeled and halved

1 tbsp plain flour

1 tsp picked, fresh thyme

1 tbsp maple syrup

4 large or 6 medium chicken breasts (with skin)

1 tbsp olive oil

100g sliced pancetta

1 tbsp wholegrain mustard

1–2 tbsp gravy granules

You will also need a large, deep sided roasting tin

Preheat the oven to 190°C/375°F/Gas Mark 5.

Bring a pan of salted water to the boil and parboil the parsnips for 5–10 minutes until they are just starting to soften. Drain, tip back in the pan and dust with the flour and thyme. Drizzle with the maple syrup and toss to coat.

Cut the chicken breasts in half, at an angle.

Add the olive oil to the roasting tin and place over the hob to heat. Once the oil is hot, add the parsnips and chicken pieces and bake in the oven for 20–25 minutes until golden brown.

Add the sliced pancetta to the roasting tin, return to the oven for another 10 minutes or until the chicken is cooked through.

Transfer the chicken, pancetta and vegetables to a serving plate with a slotted spoon and keep warm. Pour 500ml boiling water into the tin and place on the hob over a medium-high heat. Using a wooden spoon, scrape the sticky vegetable and meat juices from the bottom of the tin. Add the mustard and gravy granules and simmer until the gravy reaches your desired consistency. Serve poured over the chicken and parsnips.

CHICKEN, CHORIZO AND POTATO FRITTATA

I love chorizo - it's one of those ingredients that I always have in the fridge and it turns this humble frittata into something really special.

3 tbsp olive oil
1 tsp unsalted butter
1 red onion, finely diced
1 clove of garlic, thinly sliced
100g chorizo, diced
60g green beans, chopped
   into 3cm pieces
200g potatoes, peeled,
   cooked, cooled and sliced
130g cooked chicken, shredded
6 large eggs
50ml full-fat milk
75g Cheddar, grated
pinch of black pepper

You will also need a 25cm frying pan with an ovenproof handle

Preheat the oven to 200°C/400°F/Gas Mark 6.

Heat 1 tablespoon of the olive oil and the butter in the frying pan and add the onions. Sauté for 8-10 minutes until the onions are softened.

Add the garlic and chorizo and fry for 2–3 minutes, until the chorizo releases its amber oil.

Add the beans, potatoes and chicken and stir to coat. Add the remaining oil to prevent the frittata from sticking to the pan.

Beat the eggs together with the milk. Add 25g of the Cheddar and a pinch of black pepper. Pour into the frying pan around the chicken and chorizo mixture and top with the remaining Cheddar.

Slide the pan into the preheated oven, turn the temperature down to 190°C/375°F/Gas Mark 5, and bake for 13–16 minutes until just set and golden brown.

Leave to settle for 5 minutes before cutting into wedges. Serve warm, hot or even cold with a salad.

PORK CHOP BAKE

*Crisp crackling, soft, sticky apples: a real autumnal dish. The best thing is,
it only needs a very small amount of prep and then you pop it in the oven.
Dylan loves this with aioli mash and gravy made from the pan juices.*

8 small potatoes (preferably
    King Edwards)
2 large red onions
2 eating apples
4 tbsp olive oil
4 pork chops
pinch of sea salt
1 bulb of fennel, trimmed

**You will also need a large, deep
roasting tin and a griddle pan**

Preheat the oven to 200°C/400°F/Gas Mark 6.

Slice the potatoes (skins on) in half horizontally,
peel and chop the onions into quarters, and halve
and core the eating apples. Put everything in the
roasting tray, with half the olive oil, and stir to
coat. Place in the oven to roast for half an hour.

Meanwhile, prepare the pork chops by snipping
the rind at 1cm intervals with scissors – this will
make it go crispy when cooking – and rubbing
the meat with the remaining olive oil and salt.
Chop the fennel into wedges.

After the vegetables have been roasting for
20 minutes, place a griddle pan over a high heat
and add the chops and fennel. Cook for 3 minutes
on each side, before placing in the oven to finish
for a further 10–12 minutes depending on the
size of the chops.

TOAD IN THE HOLE

Years ago I found that if you use equal measures of each of the batter ingredients this wonderful dish will work perfectly every time – crisp on the outside and deliciously pillowy inside. I use a teacup. Another thing I learnt is to never use the sausage fat to cook the 'hole' – it just doesn't work. Remember to take out the top shelf from your oven to give it space to grow.

1 teacup plain flour
1 teacup full-fat milk
3 large eggs
pinch of salt
3 sprigs of thyme, leaves picked
8 good quality pork sausages
4 shallots, skins on, chopped in half
vegetable oil, for roasting

You will also need two 30cm, deep roasting trays

Bits & Bobs

Yorkshire puddings
See page 249 for the perfect
Yorkshire puddings recipe.

Preheat the oven to 220°C/425°F/Gas Mark 7 – remove the top shelf.

Whisk the flour, milk, eggs and salt together in a large bowl until smooth. Add the thyme and leave to rest for at least 30 minutes.

Prick the sausages and place in the roasting tray with the shallots. Bake in the preheated oven for 15–18 minutes until the sausages are lightly browned. Peel the shallots.

Take the second, clean tray and fill with the vegetable oil to a depth of about 1cm. Place in the oven until the oil is smoking hot.

Carefully pour the batter into the hot oil and add the pre-roasted sausages and thyme. Bake in the oven on the middle-low shelf for 25 minutes or until the Yorkshire pudding is golden and well risen.

SAUSAGE MEATBALLS

With a houseful of boys, this is a superb teatime treat and can be served with pasta, rice or potato wedges. When my eldest son Billy still lived at home, this would be a really quick dinner to rustle up if he was working late.

10 herb pork sausages
2 tbsp olive oil
4 sage leaves
2 red peppers
2 red onions
2 tomatoes
2 cloves of garlic
50g Gruyère, grated

You will also need a large frying pan with an ovenproof handle and a large roasting tin

Preheat the oven to 180°C/350°F/Gas Mark 4.

Skin and divide each sausage into three meatballs, so you have 30 in total. Add half the oil to the frying pan and gently fry in two batches with the whole sage leaves until the meatballs are browned. Transfer the pan to the oven and roast the meatballs for 30 minutes.

Meanwhile, deseed the peppers, peel the onions and chop all the vegetables into quarters. Tip into the roasting tin, along with the whole garlic cloves, and roast in the oven for 20–30 minutes until soft and tender.

Remove the vegetables from the oven and blitz in a food processor until smooth. Sieve the mix to remove any skins or seeds, combine with the grated Gruyère and pour the sauce over the meatballs to serve.

BAKED COD AND CARROTS WITH FENNEL SEEDS

Aniseedy fennel seeds are great enhancers to cod, and a little honey makes the carrots wonderfully sticky and sweet. Make sure the carrots start to crisp before you add the cod.

8 whole carrots,
   trimmed and peeled
knob of butter
50ml white wine
1 tbsp clear, runny honey
1 tsp fennel seeds
2 fennel bulbs
4 cod fillets (about 400g)
1 tbsp red pesto

You will also need
a roasting pan

Preheat the oven to 180°C/350°F/Gas Mark 4.

Place the carrots, butter, wine, honey and fennel seeds in the roasting pan and toss to combine. Roast in the preheated oven for 30 minutes.

Slice the fennel into thick, approximately 1cm slices and add to the roasting pan. Roast for another 20 minutes until tender.

Turn the oven up to 200°C/400°F/Gas Mark 6 and roast the vegetables for another 5 minutes.

Meanwhile, spread the cod fillets with the red pesto and place on top of the roasted carrots and fennel. Bake for a final 12 minutes or until the fish is cooked through.

SALMON EN CROUTE

Beautiful pink fish, topped with a tangy watercress sauce and encased in puff pastry, this lovely, impressive dish is great served with a rocket salad and a glass of crisp white wine.

60g watercress
150ml sour cream
finely grated zest and
    juice of 1 lemon
1 quantity of rough puff pastry
    (see page 133) or 375g
    ready-rolled puff pastry
plain flour for rolling out
2 salmon fillets (about 240g)
1 egg yolk, beaten with
    1 tbsp milk
salt and freshly ground
    black pepper

You will also need a greased baking tray

TOP TIP
If you can't find sour cream, you can make your own by blending 1 tablespooon of lemon juice with each 150ml double cream.

Place the watercress, sour cream and zest of the lemon into the bowl of a food processor and blitz until smooth. Season to taste with sea salt and pepper.

On a floured work surface, roll the pastry out to a 50 x 30cm rectangle and slice into 4 even sized rectangles measuring 25 x 15cm.

Place 2 pastry pieces on a sheet of baking parchment and position the salmon fillets on top. Spread each with a generous layer of the watercress cream.

Brush around the fillets with egg wash, place the second pieces of pastry on top and neatly tuck around the fish, removing any air bubbles and sealing the pastry together. Trim off any excess pastry and crimp the edges with a fork. Brush with egg wash and transfer to the prepared baking tray and chill for 30 minutes.

About 20 minutes before you are ready to bake the fish, preheat the oven to 200°C/400°F/Gas Mark 6.

Bake in the preheated oven for 14–18 minutes or until the pastry is golden, the bottom is crisp and the salmon is cooked through.

If you have any watercress cream left over, add lemon juice to taste and serve on the side.

Chapter
ten

TEATIME
TREATS

*When I was a little girl, we always had Sunday tea
and I loved it: 'pink fish' sandwiches (never 'tinned
salmon' as I hated it, even though when I was told
it was 'pink fish' I loved it) and one of those bought
frozen cream cakes. I still love Sunday tea but now
I just expect a little more from it. In this chapter
I'll show you how to make everything from eclairs
to Essex-style Portuguese tarts.*

CRISPY MINTY MACARONS

I made these with one of my oldest friends, Nancy, in mind. She's not a massive chocolate eater, but she loves dark chocolate, and with the mint from the Matchmakers I think they would be her perfect after-dinner treat.

60g ground almonds

15g cocoa powder

115g icing sugar

2 room-temperature large egg whites (ideally separated the night before)

50g caster sugar

Chocolate ganache

90ml double cream

60g dark chocolate, finely chopped

40g milk chocolate, finely chopped

10 Quality Street Matchmakers in cool mint (you can also use orange), crushed to rough crumbs

You will also need 1 large piping bag fitted with a plain nozzle and 2 baking trays lined with baking parchment

Blend the ground almonds, cocoa powder and icing sugar for about 30 seconds in a food processor until a fine powder. Sieve into a bowl.

In a separate large clean, dry mixing bowl, whisk the egg whites into soft peaks, then slowly add the caster sugar, beating well between each addition. Continue to whisk until firm and glossy.

Fold in the almond mixture, a third at a time, using a large metal spoon. Continue to fold in a cutting or figure-of-eight movement until combined into a smooth glossy batter.

Spoon into a piping bag and pipe 60 small 6-7cm rounds onto the prepared baking trays.

Tap the baking trays firmly on the work surface to knock out any air bubbles and leave to rest, uncovered, to form a skin, for 1 hour.

Preheat the oven to 150°C/300°F/Gas Mark 2. Bake the macarons, one tray at a time, on the middle shelf of the preheated oven for 10–12 minutes or until firm. Leave to cool on the tray for at least 10 minutes.

Make a chocolate ganache by bringing the cream to the boil in a small saucepan. Remove from the heat, then add the chopped chocolates and stir until smooth and shiny. Pour into the piping bag and leave to set in the fridge until pliable and firm.

Pipe small mounds of the ganache onto the flat side of half of the cooled macaron shells, sprinkle with the Matchmaker crumbs, then sandwich together with the remaining shells.

Store in the fridge until ready to serve.

RASPBERRY RED VELVET CAKE

I developed this fruity alternative to the more traditional red velvet cake to avoid using lots of food colouring. It's devilishly moist and rich.

160g unsalted butter, softened
280g caster sugar
3 large eggs
280g self-raising flour
75g cocoa powder
125ml buttermilk
1 tsp white wine vinegar
¼ tsp red gel food colouring
75g raspberries, puréed
   and sieved
75g full-fat cream cheese

Frosting
100g butter, softened
200g icing sugar
50g full-fat cream cheese
150g raspberries

You will also need two
20cm sandwich tins,
lightly greased and lined
with baking parchment

Preheat the oven to 180°C/350°F/Gas Mark 4.

In the bowl of a free-standing mixer, or using an electric hand-held mixer, cream the butter and sugar together until light and fluffy.

Add the eggs one at a time, beating well between each addition.

Sieve the flour and cocoa powder into a separate bowl, add half to the cake batter and gently fold in using a large metal spoon or rubber spatula.

Mix together the buttermilk, vinegar, food gel, raspberry purée and cream cheese. Add half of this mixture to the batter and gently fold in. Repeat the process with the remaining dry and wet ingredients until completely combined.

Divide the batter between the prepared sandwich tins and spread level with a palette knife.

Cook on the middle shelf of the preheated oven for 30–40 minutes until a skewer comes out clean when inserted into the middle of the cake.

Leave the cakes to cool in the tin for 10 minutes before carefully turning out onto a wire rack to cool completely.

To make the frosting, cream together the butter and icing sugar in the bowl of a free-standing mixer or with a hand-held electric whisk, until light and fluffy. Beat in the cream cheese until the mix is smooth and creamy.

Spread half the frosting on the first sandwich, sprinkle over the raspberries and top with the remaining sandwich. Spread over the rest of the frosting and smooth with a palette knife.

ORANGE, CHOCOLATE AND PRALINE MERINGUE

I was bread baking in the summer and had loads of egg whites leftover from all the egg washes. I decided to make a pavlova and the orange and chocolate worked so well with the pecan praline, along with the soft marshmallow meringue, that I had to share it with you!

Meringue
6 large egg whites
300g caster sugar
1 tsp cornflour

Filling
100g caster sugar
12 pecans
2 oranges
400ml double cream
100g milk chocolate, chopped

You will also need 2 baking trays, lined with baking parchment, or 1 lined baking tray and 1 silicone mat. Draw an 18cm circle on the baking parchment on the baking tray

TOP TIP
Always use a spotlessly clean, dry bowl when beating egg whites, as even a speck of dirt, oil or yolk will stop them becoming stiff.

Preheat the oven at 100°C/200°F/Gas Mark ½.

Whisk the egg whites to soft peaks using an electric hand whisk or free-standing mixer. Gradually add the sugar, 1 tablespoon at a time, whisking constantly until the whites come to a stiff peak. Add the cornflour and whisk again to combine.

Spoon on the meringue, keeping it within the circle lines on the parchment, building it up high and rounding off the edges with a spatula. Bake in the oven, on the middle shelf, for about 3 hours until dry and crisp. Turn the oven off and leave the meringue inside to cool.

To make the filling, gently melt the sugar with 1-2 tbsps water in a saucepan over a low heat until it dissolves. Bring to the boil until the sugar turns a deep caramel colour and then remove from the heat. Place the pecans on the second lined tray or silicone mat and pour over the caramel until they are all coated. Leave to harden and cool completely, then put the brittle in a sandwich bag and roughly crush with a rolling pin until it resembles breadcrumbs.

Zest the orange and add to the cream. Whisk to soft peaks. Peel and segment the oranges.

Melt the chocolate (see page 249).

To assemble, place the meringue on a serving plate. Spoon on the orange cream, top with orange segments and the praline brittle and drizzle with the melted chocolate.

PORTUGUESE TARTS, ESSEX-STYLE

These might not be to the traditional Portuguese recipe, but they are just pop-in-your-mouth size and have a great little crunch on the top. Making the crisp caramel might seem a lot of extra work but it really makes them look and taste special, so don't be tempted to skip!

4 large egg yolks
80g caster sugar
40g cornflour
finely grated zest of 2 oranges
550ml full-fat milk
1-2 tbsp Grand Marnier
   or Cointreau (optional)
375g ready-rolled puff pastry
1 tbsp caster sugar
1 tsp ground cinnamon

Preheat the oven to 180°C/350°F/Gas Mark 4.

Whisk the egg yolks in a bowl with the sugar, cornflour, orange zest and 90ml of the milk until smooth.

Heat the rest of the milk in a small pan until almost boiling, then pour over the egg mixture, whisking constantly. Add the liqueur, if using, return to the pan and cook over a gentle heat, whisking constantly, until the mixture boils and thickens. Simmer for a further minute to cook out the flour. Transfer to a jug to cool slightly and cover with cling film directly on the surface of the custard to stop a skin forming.

Unwrap the pastry and sprinkle over the sugar and cinnamon in an even layer. Slice the pastry into quarters and place one piece on top of another to make 2 sandwiches. Roll up each sandwich into a tight log shape and slice each log into 8 slices. Turn each disc over onto its cut side and flatten out, so that it fits into the prepared muffin moulds. Make sure there are no gaps in the pastry or the custard will leak.

Caramel
200g caster sugar
1 tsp white wine vinegar
1 tbsp water

You will also need two 12-hole muffin tins, greased with butter, and an oiled baking tray

TOP TIP
Caramel test
To test that caramel has reached the correct stage, dip a spoon into the caramel, then dip it into a glass of water. If it turns solid, the caramel is ready.

Spoon a tablespoon of custard into each tart and bake on the middle shelf of the oven for 18–22 minutes until they are risen and golden. Remove from the tin and allow to cool completely on a wire rack.

Just before serving, make the caramel by putting the sugar, vinegar and water in a pan over a medium heat. Without stirring, let the caramel turn amber in colour. Spoon over the cooled tarts in a thin layer.

ECCLES CAKES

A classic recipe but one that I learnt to make very late in life. The wonderful thing about the baking revival is that it gets us trying things we may never have tried before. Here, I've added some plump raisins – I know this might not be particularly traditional but for me it adds something special to the mix.

30g butter, unsalted
30g soft light brown
   or demerera sugar
70g caster sugar
pinch ground nutmeg
½ tsp ground cinnamon
50g candied peel paste
   (see below)
150g currants
50g raisins
1 quantity of rough puff
   pastry (see page 133)
1 egg white, beaten
2 tbsp caster sugar

You will also need a baking tray lined with baking parchment and a 12.5cm round cutter

TOP TIP
Candied peel paste is easily made by simply blending a whole tub of mixed peel in a food processor until you have a smooth paste. Store in an airtight box or jar for use as and when needed.

Warm the butter and sugars in a saucepan over a low heat, until the butter has melted and the sugar dissolved.

Tip into a bowl and add the spices, peel paste and dried fruits. Stir to combine, then set aside to cool.

Roll out the pastry between two sheets of baking parchment to the thickness of a £1 coin and cut out 8 discs (cut the discs close together to minimise waste as you can't re-roll rough puff pastry).

Divide the cooled fruit mix between the discs, leaving at least a 1cm border all around the fruit; pull the pastry up around the filling and pinch to seal in the middle. Turn each pastry over, so the pinched seal is hidden, place on the prepared baking tray and flatten slightly with the palm of your hand.

Preheat the oven to 200°C/400°F/Gas Mark 6.

Brush the cakes with the beaten egg white and sprinkle over the caster sugar. Chill for at least 15 minutes.

With a sharp knife or scissors make three slashes across each of the cakes. Bake on the middle shelf of the oven for 16–18 minutes until golden.

SAVOURY ROASTED
VEGETABLE CREAM SLICE

I know a cream slice is generally thought of as a sweet dish, but the unexpectedly tasty combination of creamy cheeses, the savoury flavours of roasted vegetables and the fresh herbs make this a deliciously vibrant bake. You can either use chiller cabinet or jarred veggies.

1½ quantities of rough puff
    pastry (see page 133) or 560g
    ready-rolled puff pastry
1 egg, beaten with 1 tbsp milk
500g full-fat cream cheese
250g ricotta
small handful each of chopped
    herbs (I used basil and chives,
    but you could use any soft
    herbs such as chervil, flat-
    leaf parsley, coriander,
    lemon thyme)
freshly grated zest
    of 1 small lemon
pinch of freshly ground
    black pepper
250g roasted artichoke
    hearts, drained
250g sunblush tomatoes,
    drained
250g roasted peppers, drained

**You will also need 2 baking trays
lined with baking parchment**

Preheat the oven to 200°C/400°F/Gas Mark 6.

Lightly flour your work surface and roll out the pastry if using homemade. Cut the pastry into three 20 x 27cm pieces, place on the lined trays, prick with a fork and brush with the egg wash. Bake in the oven for 12–14 minutes or until risen and golden. Remove from the trays and leave to cool on a wire rack.

Mix together the cream cheese, ricotta, herbs, lemon zest and pepper until well combined.

Drain the vegetables from the olive oil. Cut the artichoke hearts and roasted peppers into pieces the same size as the sunblush tomatoes.

Spread half the mixture over the first pastry tile, then layer with half the artichokes, sunblush tomatoes and roasted peppers. Top with the second pastry tile, repeat with the remaining cream cheese mix and roasted vegetables and sandwich with the final tile.

ASPARAGUS TIPS WRAPPED IN PARMA HAM

I love English asparagus and I love that I inherited a big patch with my garden. Wrapped in a wonderful salty cured ham, with a drizzle of oil and a splash of lemon juice, these simple savoury bites are a real treat to behold.

24 asparagus tips
4 tbsp extra virgin olive oil
juice of 1 lemon
black pepper
6 slices of Parma ham
  (about 90g)

You will also need a flat griddle pan or solid-based non-stick frying pan

Heat a flat griddle pan or non-stick frying pan over a low heat. Drizzle 1 tablespoon of the olive oil over the asparagus tips and cook until charred and tender. Leave to cool.

Whisk the remaining oil, lemon juice and black pepper together to make a dressing and pour over the asparagus.

Tear the slices of Parma ham in half, to create 12 pieces, and wrap each around 2 of the tips. Serve drizzled with any remaining dressing.

STRIPY STRAWBERRY AND VANILLA SWISS ROLL

This cake really has the wow factor and will make a very impressive centrepiece to any table. You could change the colour to blue if you are baking for a boy, and make polka dots instead of stripes. Either way, make the coloured sponge mix first so you can freeze it.

Pink sponge
70g unsalted butter, softened
70g caster sugar
¼ tsp 'hot pink' gel
   food colouring
70g flour
2 large egg whites

Swiss roll
4 large eggs
100g caster sugar
100g self-raising flour

In the bowl of a free-standing mixer, or using an electric hand-held mixer, cream the butter and sugar together until light and fluffy. Add the food colouring, mix again and then fold in the flour until just combined.

In a separate, spotlessly clean, dry bowl, whisk the egg whites together until doubled in volume and will hold a peak. Fold into the cake batter using a large metal spoon and spoon the mix into the piping bag. Pipe diagonal lines (interspersed with dots or your chosen design), across the prepared baking tray and place in the freezer for 20 minutes.

Preheat the oven to 180ºC/350ºF/Gas Mark 4.

Make the Swiss roll by whisking the eggs and caster sugar together in a free-standing mixer until pale, doubled in volume, light and fluffy.

Using a large metal spoon fold in the flour, one third at a time. Carefully pour over the frozen coloured batter and spread level with a palette knife.

Filling
500ml double cream
1 tsp vanilla bean paste
3 heaped tbsp strawberry jam
300g strawberries, hulled
   and halved

You will also need a piping
bag fitted with a plain nozzle,
and a 40 x 28cm Swiss roll
tin, well-greased and lined

Bake on the middle shelf of the preheated oven for 12–15 minutes until golden and springy to the touch. Carefully transfer to a wire rack, peel back the parchment paper and allow to cool for 5 minutes. Cover with a damp tea towel.

Whisk the double cream until it forms soft peaks and swirl in the jam.

Turn the cooled Swiss roll back over on to the damp tea towel, making sure the pink pattern is facing down. Spread with the cream and top neatly with the sliced strawberries.

Roll it up, starting at one of the shorter ends and using the tea towel to help support you and transfer onto a serving plate.

BANOFFEE ECLAIRS

A twist on an old favourite. My auntie always used to bring along traditional eclairs on a Saturday, when we visited our Nanny Jess, so these remind me of her.

⅓ quantity choux pastry
   (see page 134)
1 ice cube
2 bananas
300ml double cream

Filling
100g soft dark brown sugar
80ml double cream
30g unsalted butter

Topping
150g dark chocolate
1tbsp golden syrup
20g unsalted butter

You will also need a large
baking tray lined with baking
parchment and 2 disposable
piping bags

Preheat the oven to 190°C/375°F/Gas Mark 5.

Spoon the choux pastry into a piping bag and pipe 7–8cm long eclairs on the lined baking tray, leaving plenty of space on the tray for them to spread. Place an ice cube in a small baking dish in the base of the preheated oven to create some steam and bake on the middle shelf for 15 minutes. until golden and puffed up.

Remove the eclairs from the oven and slice them lengthways in half. Return to the oven for 5 minutes to allow the inside of the eclairs to dry, then leave to cool completely on a wire rack.

Mash the bananas until smooth. Whip the double cream until it forms medium-firm peaks and combine with the bananas. Spoon into a piping bag and chill for 30 minutes.

To make the toffee filling, heat the sugar, double cream and butter together in a saucepan until the sugar has dissolved. Bring to the boil and reduce the sauce by a third stirring from time to time. Pour into a shallow bowl and chill for 30 minutes or until set to a spreadable consistency.

Snip the end of the piping bag and pipe the banana cream into each of the eclairs, followed by the toffee. Return the eclairs to the fridge and chill for 10 minutes.

Melt the dark chocolate, golden syrup and butter in a heatproof bowl in the microwave on a low setting, stir to combine then spread over the chilled eclairs with a palette knife and leave to set.

Teatime treats

BITS & BOBS

Flavoured shortbread

Try adding lemon or orange zest for a fruity twist, chocolate chips, or sprinkle over flaked almonds before baking.

Savoury pretzels

If you prefer your pretzels to have a savoury kick, follow my recipe on page 48 but substitute the ground cinnamon sugar at the end with chilli salt. You can buy this ready mixed, but you can also make your own by blitzing sea salt and dried chilli flakes together in a food processor.

Cheat's crystallised citrus fruits

Zest 2 citrus fruits (lemon, lime or orange) into long strips, boil for 10 minutes in water, drain and boil for another 15 minutes in 100ml water and 80g sugar. Drain and transfer to baking parchment. Sprinkle with 2 tablespoons granulated sugar and leave to dry. Once dried, store in an air-tight jar. Try sprinkling over other desserts, such as a crème brûlée.

Rosemary oil

You can make this yourself by inserting 2-3 large sprigs of rosemary into a bottle of olive or rapeseed oil and leaving it to infuse for 2–4 days. Keep the oil in the fridge and make sure it is topped up in the bottle so that the rosemary is always covered.

Chocolate ganache

Pour 200m double cream into a pan and bring to the boil, remove from the heat, then add 150g good quality dark chocolate amd 50g milk chocolate that's been roughly chopped. Stir until smooth and shiny. Chill until firm. Whisk until light, fluffy and pale in colour, then spoon into a piping bag.

Macerated sultanas

Heat together 100g sultanas, the juice of 1 orange (remove the zest first), 1 shot of Cointreau (obviously not for children) and 3 heaped tablespoons caster sugar in a pan, and let it bubble until it becomes syrupy. Add the zest of the orange and leave to cool.

Poached pears

Put 250 ml water, 60g caster sugar and the peel of half an orange into a saucepan and bring to the boil. Add three small peeled dessert pears and cover. Poach the fruit in the sugar syrup, along with a split vanilla pod, for around 12–15 minutes until completely cooked through (timing will depend on the ripeness of the fruit). Serve with vanilla or chocolate ice cream and a sprinkling of toasted hazelnuts.

Grown-up frittata

I've kept my frittata recipe on page 22 simple to keep children happy but to make a more grown-up version, try topping them with 1–2 tablespoons flaked almonds and/or grated Parmesan cheese.

Butterscotch

Gently heat 200g soft light brown sugar, 150ml double cream and 30g butter in a small non-stick saucepan until the sugar and butter have dissolved completely. Reduce for 2 minutes, then pour into a shallow dish and chill for 2 hours.

Pear, walnut and watercress salad

Peel, core and quarter 2 Conference pears and toss in lemon juice. Combine with 100g watercress and a handful of walnuts. In a jar, mix 120ml olive oil, 1 tablespoon wholegrain mustard and 1 tablespoon runny honey. Drizzle over the salad. Any leftover dressing will last in the fridge for a week.

Steak, red pepper and mozzarella empanadas

Fry a small piece of fillet steak with half a roasted red pepper (you can get these jarred) in 1 teaspoon of olive oil. Allow to cool, then mix with 3 tablespoons of grated mozzarella and follow the instructions for empanadas on page 143.

Sweet pastry straws

As a chef's treat, and to avoid waste, take any scraps of puff pastry, sprinkle with sugar and ground cinnamon, and twist into sweet pastry straws. Bake in the oven for 8–10 minutes until puffed up and golden.

Brandy butter

Place 100g softened unsalted butter, 2 tablespoons icing sugar and 2 tablespoons brandy into a food processor and blitz until smooth. Spoon into a bowl, cover with cling film and chill until needed.

White chocolate hearts

Carefully melt 50g white chocolate in a sandwich bag in the microwave on a low heat in 10-second bursts. Snip the end of the sandwich bag and use it like a piping bag to create heart shapes on baking parchment. Chill until set.

Yorkshire puddings

Whether making a clafoutis or Yorkshire puddings for the Sunday roast, I always use the same proportions for the batter. Just remember – 1 teacup plain flour, 1 teacup whole milk and 1 teacup of eggs (about 3 large ones). Whisk until smooth and give it time to rest before using.

The perfect meringue

The trick to getting the perfect meringue is to use older eggs rather than fresh, and separate the whites from the yolks as far in advance as possible (ideally overnight).

Melted chocolate

A great way to melt chocolate, especially if you are using it to drizzle, is in a sandwich bag in the microwave. Melt it in 20-second bursts on a low setting to make sure it doesn't burn.

Salted caramel

For a delicioius topping for ice cream gently heat 200g soft light brown sugar, 150ml double cream, 30g unsalted butter and 1 tsp salt in a pan until the sugar and butter has dissolved. Bring to the boil, reduce the heat to a simmer and reduce for 2 minutes until thickened, then pour into a shallow dish and chill for 2 hours.

INDEX

ACKNOWLEDGEMENTS

There are so many wonderful people I need to thank for all their help in making my second book a reality.

Firstly I'd like to thank Andreas, Charlotte and everyone at Constable & Robinson for all their support, belief and hard work (and of course taste testing in 'The Office'!). Phil and Sharon, thank you for your continued belief.

To Fiona, Ally and everyone at Limelight: thank you for always looking out for me.

To Alex, Emma and the Smith and Gilmour team: you are the BEST design team.

To Sairey for my gorgeous outfit choices. And Liz you made the impossible happen making me look fab. Please come and live with me.

For Jesse, Jude, Harley, Lily, Grace and my boys, thank you for the days modelling.

For Laura: you made it a breeze, thanks hun. To Annie, Rachel, Kathryn and Kim for all your hard work in the kitchen. To Lydia for your lovely things. Mungo I love you.

For Martin: not only do you always without fail find the most fantastic shot, along with Penfold you crack me up every day we work together. And to Gina for working tirelessly.

To my little family, Richard, Billy, Jesse and Dylan: thank you for the pride I see on your faces when I have a new project on the go.